ITALIAN LOUISIANA

HISTORY, HERITAGE & TRADITION

ALAN G. GAUTHREAUX

Foreword by D.G. HIPPENSTEEL, PhD

Charleston London

THE
History
PRESS

Published by The History Press
Charleston, SC 29403
www.historypress.net

First published 2014

Manufactured in the United States

ISBN 978.1.62619.385.7

Library of Congress CIP data applied for.

This book is dedicated to
Richard and Evelyn Gauthreaux, my parents;
Alvin A. LeBlanc, my maternal grandfather;
and Joan L. Strahan, mother-in-law, grandmother and mother.

Contents

Foreword

Beauty is truth, truth beauty,—that is all
Ye know on earth, and all ye need to know.
—John Keats

In our postmodern time, it is rare to find truth in history. It is also rare to discover any niche of American history that has not been unearthed, over-commented on and subjected to multiple and continued revisionist perspectives, thereby essentially burying the truth and significance of the historical moment. It is rarer still to have a heretofore unknown historical American moment escape the eye of a historian.

Yet Alan Gauthreaux's *Italian Louisiana* is just such a rare and remarkable find of beauty and truth. *Italian Louisiana* is at once an impeccable historical research project but stylized as a popular and interesting historical narrative. Unearthing the struggles of Italian immigrants in the historical moment of the post–Civil War era to the 1920s, Gauthreaux becomes more than an incredible historian but also a highly competent criminologist and a master storyteller. This work places Gauthreaux in the company of Richard Gambino, Humbert S. Nelli, Vincenza "Jean" Scarpaci, David McCullough and Gordon S. Wood.

The underlying gripping and complex saga of Gauthreaux's historical moment not only informs the reader through traditional historical fare but also chronicles riveting accounts of individual and mass criminal behavior that rivals today's cinematic and televised productions.

Gauthreaux paints such vivid and detailed mental pictures that the reader becomes one of the participants in a mob on its way to lynching eleven imprisoned Italians. The reader's own heart races as if one of the Italians fleeing and fighting to escape the inevitable. The author has the reader playing detective and criminologist as the story of Louisiana's first recorded serial killer is pieced together.

Italian Louisiana includes not only these eye-popping micro-histories embedded in the overarching historical moment; Gauthreaux also remains true to the tenets of all great historical analyses as he masterfully unveils the frailty, resilience, hope and strength of the human endeavor in a world of evil and chaos.

Gauthreaux's work is also a masterful piece of macro-history. Through the facts, he is able to relate the heart-rending experiences of American immigration from a new and refreshing perspective—the unique Louisiana culture. *Italian Louisiana* explores the dual nature of humanity through the struggle of Italian assimilation. The fabric in which Gauthreaux's historical moment is woven is that of man's inhumanity to man and the ultimate Italian response to that inhumanity. The author weaves many threads into that historical fabric: racism, ignorance, justice and injustice; at the same time, the author maintains focus on the prize—the Italian community never wavers in believing in freedom and its eventual acceptance into the landscape of the American dream. In the pattern of the fabric created by Gauthreaux, we see our own moral selves, our ever-deliberate but positive progress toward equity as a people and a nation and our own daily struggles as we choose between right and wrong, good and evil.

Italian Louisiana is more than just a meticulously researched, previously unknown historical moment, more than just a masterful story told anew; it also takes the beauty and truth of that historical moment and engages us today across the chasm of time and place.

As a criminologist, a current law enforcement officer and an amateur historian, it is fascinating for me to have Alan G. Gauthreaux, who is a consummate historian and excellent criminologist, as a colleague and a friend. I am humbled and honored that my colleague and friend offered me this opportunity to comment on this unforgettable work. It is my hope that I have been faithful to that trust.

D.G. HIPPENSTEEL, PhD
Assistant Professor of Criminal Justice
Delgado Community College
New Orleans
September 2013

Preface

I wrote the present manuscript as a discovery of truth after several years of research. For a long time, I have been interested in the Italian immigrants who settled in Louisiana without sharing that heritage myself. Contrary to my initial reservations, the Italian people opened their hearts so that an accurate record of their ancestors' plight in Louisiana would be objectively portrayed without the conjecture and assumptions that constantly purvey an outsider's understanding of their experiences.

Contained within these pages is that story of Italians in Louisiana: their arrival in the New World and the obstacles they faced from a political, cultural and ethnic perspective that have been considerably downplayed in Louisiana history—until now.

Over ten years ago, I began this journey not knowing what to expect. Through interviews with Italians in New Orleans and the surrounding areas, research in archives and museums and observance of various Italian and Sicilian festivals around Louisiana, I realized that the Italian people are truly unique. If some consider this work to have pro-Italian undertones, then there is a lack of understanding of Italian culture and, more importantly, of Italian people as a whole. Any advocacy for the Italian people portrayed within these pages is merely incidental to the events related within this work. To know their history, one must delve deeper, past the accepted stereotype of the Italian people. This manuscript may briefly mention the criminal facet of the Italian experience in Louisiana, but positive focus was maintained on the more historically significant events.

Italian Louisiana concentrates on a historical analysis of these Mediterranean people and their interaction with the populations of Louisiana. The Italian people are very proud of their heritage and that of their ancestors. The negative stereotypes from their past have created nothing but animosity among Italians toward historians and those who accept societal portrayals of a criminal underclass. The openness they exhibited with me toward my inquiries came with the stipulation that their story be told with all correctness and accuracy. I have attempted to do this with their kind assistance and patience.

Alan G. Gauthreaux
August 2013

Acknowledgements

I would like to acknowledge, first and foremost, my wife, Lisa, and my daughter, Mia Adeline, without whose support, encouragement and patience I would never have succeeded in writing this manuscript.

A few others helped me with the support and production of this work as well: Dr. Daryl G. Hippensteel, professor of criminal justice and head of the criminal justice center at Delgado Community College, a great mentor, friend and colleague; Mr. Angelo J. Spinato Jr., who helped me to better understand Italian culture in New Orleans; Ms. Regina Bertolino, president, East Jefferson Italian American Society; Ms. Silva Blake, assistant archivist at the Historic New Orleans Collection; Ms. Leah Huett and Ms. Judy Bolton at LSU Libraries, Hill Memorial Library, Manuscript Section; the Microform Collection at Earl K. Long Library, University of New Orleans; the Louisiana Collection at the Jefferson Parish Public Library; the late Mr. Joseph Maselli, Italian American advocate; Mr. Sal Serio Sr., curator of oral histories, American Italian Cultural Center in New Orleans; Ms. Irene Wainwright, head archivist at the Louisiana Collection/City Archives housed at the New Orleans Public Library, Loyola Branch; Ms. Melody Vaughan White, for her thoughtful critiques and artistic ideas; and finally, Mr. Richard Jay Gauthreaux, my brother and constant source of encouragement.

Introduction

O n March 14, 1891, at approximately 11:00 a.m., the area surrounding the Orleans Parish Prison resembled bloody battlefields reminiscent of the Civil War some thirty years past. Two bodies hung from the lamppost and tree immediately adjacent to the destroyed gates of the prison, the blood from their wounds dripping into puddles beneath them. Just inside the prison gates, six men received over one hundred gunshot wounds, mostly to the head, their bodies laid in a neat row for a display of the horrific work done to them by the mob. Three more men lay dead in a corridor inside the prison and suffered the same fate as those in the prison yard. The wounds to all the bodies displayed a vengeful animosity that exceeded the hatred of a thousand hearts. The only crime committed by these men was that they were Italian.

The killing of the eleven Italians by a mob estimated at more than five thousand took less than twenty minutes. In that time, although they had been found innocent of murdering a highly respected lawman, the legal system failed the decedents, and those twenty minutes still reverberate through United States history as the country's worst mass killing of all time. This brutal execution forced Italy to defend her countrymen with a serious threat of war against the United States, and when diplomatic wrangling finally concluded, the United States capitulated and paid the deceased men's families an indemnity; a small price to pay for the crime of murder, given the anti-Italian atmosphere at the time.

This single event that occurred on March 14, 1891, defined the treatment of Italians in Louisiana for over five generations. Their struggles in a new land contained more than just tales of the immigrant experience in a strange country; they were a story of survival in a hostile environment based on their ethnic background and their inability to conform to the prejudices of whites. Even to the present day, this one event still defines what most people know about Italians in the area.

As difficult as the journey to the New World may have been for the poor Italians, the societal adjustments once they arrived in Louisiana appeared minimal. As time went on, however, and realizing that southern Italians' experiences with their northern Italian neighbors may have prepared them for any further prejudices, associating with African Americans seemed harmless. The white perception that Italians would supplement the population and thereby gain some majority over the blacks in Louisiana was dispelled. Italians felt no animosity toward blacks because nothing in their past prepared them for a prejudice based solely on skin color. This led the immigrants to conduct business with blacks only because both races realized that white planters chicaned them when it came to negotiating for farming supplies and harvested produce. Subsequently, this reciprocity among blacks and Italians angered white natives; so much so that whites considered Italians "Negroes with white skin."

In addition to their associations with blacks in Louisiana, the Italians were seen as economic competition, which contributed greatly to anti-Italian sentiment in areas such as New Orleans and Tangipahoa Parish. Before 1890, this perceived economic competition played no part in the prejudice against them, and whites believed that Italian immigrants assisted greatly with the economic vigor that revived New Orleans as a major port after the Civil War. However, approaching the twentieth century, Italians were considered to be in competition with white merchants and planters. Italian workers were not as passive as was first thought, and Italians worked toward an equal social standing with whites. This infuriated whites and reignited nativist sympathies that had first surfaced in America during the 1850s.

Subsequently, the thought of Italians seeking equal social status with whites offended the latter's sense of class distinction. The Italians exhibited providence with their earnings, sending a great portion of their salaries home to families left behind in Italy in the hopes of bringing those family members to the United States or assisting them financially. In sending money out of the country, this ensured that the Louisiana economy would not significantly benefit from the Italians' labor. One distinguished American politician of the time, Henry Cabot Lodge, stated that Italians "form an element in the population with regards as home a foreign country, instead of that in which they live and earn money. They have no interest or stake in the country, and they become American citizens." This assertion of abandoning the economy for the benefit of helping relatives enhanced nativist beliefs against the Italians in Louisiana and convinced whites that Italians just did not belong in their society. Some whites believed that sending wages home allegedly proved detrimental to local businesses that depended on the Italians' skills to stay in business. Louisiana entrepreneurs, then, by the 1890s, began to reestablish faith in African American laborers because they tended to indulge themselves locally, "spending more money than they earned." This perception on behalf of whites proved incorrect, as presently many Italian businesses in Louisiana have survived as a result of ancestral frugality. Italians believed they were doing the right and honorable thing in supporting relatives in their homeland. What whites refused to see was the Italian dedication to family: a loyalty stronger than any economic tether. Unfortunately, nativists drew strength from a paranoid perception and the stereotype of foreigners.

The sentiment exhibited against Italians in Louisiana eventually subsided but has never been forgotten. Within these pages lies not just another rendition of their story but a more elaborative documentation of the tales often told in Italian families for more than five generations. Some of these stories are still too painful for Italians to mention in mixed company, but eventually the difficult history of Italian immigration to Louisiana gave way to their subsequent assimilation into Louisiana society, as well as American society.

After studying the Italian experience, one must ask if the years of sacrifice produced the desired result. The response lies in the accomplishments of those who ventured into the unknown and demonstrated the perseverance to succeed. This is their story.

Chapter 1

Il Sogno Americano

(The American Dream)

There is no room in this country for hyphenated Americans…There is no such thing as a hyphenated American who is a good American.
—*Theodore Roosevelt, October 1915, Knights of Columbus Meeting, Carnegie Hall*

At the end of the American Civil War in 1865, the southern economy lay in ruin and thousands of freed black slaves sought to exercise their newly granted freedom. For years, plantation owners had denied them formal education. Once freedom finally came, many of the former slaves searched for livelihoods. Freed blacks still found themselves connected to the land and engaged in a tenant relationship with the homesteads they once toiled in bondage. Louisiana planters feared that their tenants would abandon their fields and leave crops to be harvested without the workforce to complete the task. This labor uncertainty plagued Louisiana planters, who found it imperative to find workers to complete the task at hand.

Radical Reconstruction enhanced the devastation brought on by the Civil War to the South, partly from an economic point of view but most certainly along political and racial lines. The economic collapse of southern markets without free labor to replace slavery seemed certain, but by the mid-1860s, Louisiana planters prepared not only to secure field workers willing to replace black labor but also to procure a ready-made labor force in the Mediterranean area of Europe—and the means to increase the white population of the South to combat Radical Reconstruction. Although the idea of recruiting labor from Southern Europe seemed to resolve this problem, influential white citizens—wealthy planters or those who owned businesses—of Louisiana could not have imagined how it misjudged the racial and ethnic proclivities of the new immigrants. Unaware of the prejudices that existed in the South, but suffering under similar intolerances in their own land, southern Italians sought a land where their stations would change without the fear of heavy taxation and famine. More importantly, the immigrants longed for an opportunity to prosper.

The Italians first set foot in Louisiana in the sixteenth century. The many stages of European exploration provided opportunities for adventure seekers willing to risk a perilous journey across the Atlantic Ocean in the hopes of finding wealth and prosperity. Italians first came to this continent in 1540, as the De Soto expedition that ventured into the Mississippi River Valley contained Cristofaro de Spinola, a captain from Hidalgo, Spain, and a Genoese adventurer named Bernado Peloso. De Spinola later married the daughter of a conquistador. Over one hundred years later, Henri de Tonti, or Enrico de Tonti, a native of Naples, made his way with La Salle to the lower Mississippi River Valley.

The French founded New Orleans in 1718 and steadily populated the colony. Among the foreigners who first came to the settlement—Germans, Swiss, Irish and English—the Italians took their place. Several Italian "undesirables" were recorded in the New Orleans area as "deserters from the army and tobacco smugglers," but this did not deter further wayfarers from inhabiting the colony. For the 150 years following the first settlement, Italian immigrants slowly cascaded into the colony, arriving as soldiers who intermarried with the French or Spanish women during successive regimes. One of these military men, Francesca Maria del Reggio of Alba, Piedmont, rose to the rank of captain in the Royal Genoese Grenadiers and was assigned a command in Louisiana in October 1750. Captain del Reggio married a French woman named Helené and lived the rest of his life in the colony. His great-grandson, P.G.T. Beauregard, fired the first shots of the Civil War at Fort Sumter on April 12, 1861.

The greatest migration of Italians occurred after 1865, but circumstances that dictated their exodus from the Mediterranean nation warrant a more detailed examination of events that occurred in the nineteenth century.

Although Napoleon Bonaparte conquered much of Europe (including Italy) in the early nineteenth century, the middle classes of Italy appreciated the principles of the French Revolution—*egalité, fraternitié, liberté*—because they released the people of various governmental domains from any loyalty to local administrations. The French ruled the various duchies and municipalities of Italy from 1796 until 1814. The Italians disliked French rule but much less so than the Spanish. Even though Napoleon failed to unify Italy, Italians realized the possibility of future attempts at bringing the country together.

When Napoleon fell from power in 1815, European nation-states attempted consolidation under the Congress of Vienna. As a result, the Austrian empire wielded power over a vast empire that included much of Eastern Europe and Italy. Native Italians ruled only one state within Italy at the time (the kingdom of Sardinia, sometimes referred to as Piedmont or Savoy). On the Italian peninsula, peasants struggled against government oppression. Impoverished farmers in southern Italy and Sicily hoped to improve conditions for themselves and their families, but the revolutions that swept the landscape and later civil war, repressive taxes, inequitable land distribution policies and the constant threat of ruthless landlords forced southern Italians to rely on the tales of opportunity available to hardworking people in America.

Beginning with the demise of Napoleon's empire and the attempts of the Congress of Vienna to control territories from afar, Italians envisaged a unified state reminiscent of the Roman Empire and the Renaissance. Known as the *Risorgimento*, this ideal came to light prior to the revolutions that gripped Europe in 1848 but died as the Austrian empire reasserted its authority. It surfaced again at the end of the 1850s, when Italians again dreamed of a land free from foreign rule.

The concerted effort toward the revival of unification occurred in the state of Piedmont, ruled by King Victor Emmanuel under a constitutional monarchy since 1848. Victor Emmanuel appointed Cammilio Bonso, Count di Cavour, as his new prime minister in 1852. Cavour implemented a liberal policy for encouraging Italy's unification where Piedmont would become the measurement foundation for the ideal government. Cavour exerted great effort to convince the people of Piedmont of the necessity of incorporating democratic practices within the framework of government. In 1860, Giuseppe Garibaldi, a revolutionary with the foresight of a statesman, organized a small army, the "Red Shirts," and invaded the island of Sicily. Cavour figured he could use the revolutionary agitation Garibaldi fomented to unite the entire kingdom under his beloved Piedmont.

After conquering the island of Sicily, Garibaldi turned his attention to central Italy. His army soon marched up the peninsula toward Naples, where he expected to face a Piedmontese army. Although Garibaldi had at one time opposed a monarchy for Italy, ultimately he deduced that the best way to achieve his goal of a united Italy would be to cast his anti-monarchial sentiments aside and ally himself with Victor Emmanuel.

Subsequently, all the Italian domains except for Rome and Venetia voted to join Piedmont in the unification of Italy under King Victor Emmanuel. In order to accomplish his goals, Cavour needed the added strength of an ally to finally expel the Austrians from the peninsula. He sought to partner the Italians with the newly established empire of Napoleon III, enlisting French troops to help with the expulsion. Napoleon III agreed to the alliance because he, like other Frenchmen, believed Italy to be the ancestral home of Napoleonism. The armies of Napoleon III and the Piedmontese defeated the Austrians at the Battles of Magento and Solferino in northern Italy in 1861. This ignited an additional series of revolutions in Italy where the revolutionaries demanded unification under the Piedmont government. However, Napoleon III, responding to pressure on the homefront from Catholics, made a separate peace with the Austrians and forced Cavour to rely on plebiscites to expel the old rulers from Tuscany, Modena, Parma and Romagna. Eventually, Piedmont annexed several provinces. The one obstacle to total unification was the south—the Kingdom of the Two Sicilies—an island ripe with corruption and disloyal citizens to the standing government.

Italians in the north and the south immediately suffered the after-effects of unification, and this exposed a deeply rooted bias between the people of the two regions. Northern Italians held disdain for their neighbors in the south because of the latter's dismal economic predicament and reliance on religious guidance from clerics. Thus, northern Italians considered those from southern Italy to be uncivilized. Southern Italians considered their northern counterparts to be elitist and oppressive. Although Italians proclaimed themselves unified to the rest of the world, Sicily became the land of the outlaw. The revolutions Garibaldi conducted in Sicily and the south continued, as did the class struggle between the people of northern and southern Italy, including Sicily.

Most of the major events resulting in the Italian unification process occurred in the south; most importantly, an 1861 peasant revolt in Sicily actually threatened unification efforts. Northern Italians embraced the new government with open arms but viewed southern Italy and Sicily as backward and a hindrance to truly achieving a national identity of their own. Crime and poverty prevailed in the south as unification prevented any type of industrial progress. Economic depression accompanied unification as Italy saw an increase in its poor population when the new Cavour government freed political prisoners. Southern Italy suffered from peasant "land hunger" even before unification, and with the merger of Italy's separate parts, the peasants' situation worsened.

Count di Cavour's government sought to bring southern Italy into the fold with the rest of the country, if not with ideological persuasion then with physical force. In 1865, Cavour sent troops to southern Italy and Sicily in an attempt to control the uprisings that occurred against the new government. Italian citizens, both northern and southern, expressed uncertainty about the actual course of the government bent on dragging Italy into the Industrial Age. Like his northern supporters, Cavour considered the south to be backward and an impediment to developing a more economically and politically stable nation. Southern Italians grew distrustful of Cavour's government because of new economic platforms that threatened ruin to many southern Italian manufacturing concerns; more specifically, the peasant farmers who harvested the south's grain felt especially threatened. The more military action the government ordered, the more the civilian populations tended to resist. Numerous arrests led to prison overcrowding, which, in turn, led to mandatory releases. These parolees, unable to find gainful employment due to the struggling economy, joined roaming bands of criminals and terrorized the countryside.

The troubles that plagued the Cavour government after unification stemmed from an inability to control a population whose livelihood depended on agrarian freedom. Clearly, the southern populations of Italy, mostly Sicily, struggled to exist beneath the control of a wealthy and powerful faction. Sicilian peasants not only endured the whims of a distant administration but also paid exorbitant rents to non-attendant property owners whose overseers—*gabellotti*—took further liberties with peasants without fear of retribution. Moreover, impoverished farmers followed a course that led to further indebtedness to rich landowners. Uneven land distribution, heavy taxes, ruthless deforestation and depletion of soil through flooding and erosion caused the peasant economy to collapse. Climatic and geographic changes caused a Mediterranean "Dust Bowl," so to speak, rendering the soil into arid sand lacking nutrients enough to sustain any crops. A rise in the production of lemons and oranges internationally led to a decline in world prices that affected Italy's cash crops. With the Italian economy practically bankrupt and the majority of its population in poverty, the Cavourian dream of modernization led to failure. Even after unification seemed complete, southern Italians were disillusioned with their new masters. Many looked west, across the Atlantic Ocean, for relief from their impoverishment.

Italy gave the appearance of unification under the guise of an indigenous government, but its economy continued to struggle. The middle class hesitated to venture into foreign commerce. Instead of directing investments toward manufacturing and industry, government officials chose to rely on the rents collected from land revenues, which proved quite handsome at the time. The lack of skilled labor also played an integral part of the economic stagnation in the region. Silk grown in Sicily faced stiff competition for markets as consumers found Chinese silk cheaper and goods produced in Sicily garnered high export taxes due to the smuggling of raw silk from the island.

The winemaking regions of Italy also failed as the country's vineyards suffered in the 1870s from *phylloxera*, a plant lice that destroyed grapes. The origins of the disease traced back to the Alps in France, where it destroyed vineyards and produced very little, making the crop yield very low. In the 1880s, France issued a tariff on Italian wines and prohibited the peninsula from exporting a once reliable commodity on which Italy had heavily depended.

In addition to the weakened trade system, Italy's only partially industrialized economy contributed to the lack of stability. Industry operated in the north, while the south, with its abject poverty, relied on agriculture for survival. Due to the new unified government's insistence on promoting more industry in the north, it placed tariffs on goods produced in the south. In turn, this caused prices to plummet, forcing factories to close and workers into unemployment in the Mezzogiorno, or southern region of Italy. Thus, by attempting to promote industry to boost the economy, the new Italian government created an agricultural workforce glut that could not survive under the new principles of unification.

Military conscription also took its toll on the peasant class of southern Italy and Sicily. Peasants saw military service as the government's way of protecting those more privileged than they. They also believed that the government viewed them as cannon fodder on the battlefield. The peasant class had even less respect for the landed gentry who served mostly as officers in command of those of the lesser classes. Peasants felt that their government acted indifferently toward the deaths of their men. This apathy toward the lesser-class foot soldier translated uniformly off the battlefield as well.

The agrarian society in southern Italy and Sicily relied heavily on these peasants who had no guarantee of job stability or productive crops. The landowning class there did not appear to have any concern for the caste that provided their wealth. Under the *latifundi*, a land management system controlled by the privileged few, the Sicilian peasant languished under a tenancy existence. The peasants, the *contadini*, worked for land barons who hired overseers, the *gabellotti*, to manage their holdings. These land managers unmercifully robbed the *contadini* of their earnings through rent collections. Where the *Risorgimento* benefited the burgeoning middle class, the impoverished farmer could only hope that his support of a united Italy would bring him happiness. Even though promises of agrarian reform in the southern regions brought some sense of contentment to the lower classes after unification, peasants still suffered from the same inequitable land distribution and repressive government taxation. Moreover, Italy's population grew while its food supply lessened. The lower classes did not benefit from the *Risorgimento*, and even though Garibaldi promised the even distribution of land among the peasants, reforms did not occur as hoped. The best prospect for improving their station would be to leave their homelands and find a better life somewhere else.

As Italy struggled with the growing pains of unification and Italian peasants agonized over their options to improve their position, the United States struggled with its own re-unification after 1865. More specifically, landed whites in Louisiana sought to revert to their former antebellum identity. Planters in Louisiana argued that freed slaves would migrate to the North and West, and if the South were to re-create its society and rebuild its economy, inexpensive labor had to be secured in order to ensure the recovery. Louisiana's white planters began the active pursuit of foreigners in an attempt to fill the perceived labor void left by the newly freed blacks. Democratic political machinations also worked to restore the white power structure as planters planned the white takeover of the state with Italian and Sicilian immigrants as their enhancement to the Louisiana white electorate.

Close examination of the U.S. census from the years 1860 and 1870 fails to substantiate the planters' claims of a desperate labor shortage resulting from the migration of black laborers to other parts of the country. A total of 18,647 blacks resided in Louisiana in the year 1860, and that population exploded by 1870, growing exponentially over the next ten years. In the subsequent censuses, the black population leveled at a little over 50 percent per decade, ending in 1910. Those interested in returning Louisiana to antebellum white-dominated society sought an alliance with a new ethnic group they thought they could control politically. Into this racial and political quagmire, Italians would enter the country and state in droves without any suspicion about the motives of their hosts.

In order to implement a plan to invite European foreigners to the state, the Louisiana legislature created the Bureau of Immigration on March 17, 1866, headed first by J.C. Kathman. This bureau examined various aspects of inviting European immigrants to Louisiana in order to supplant the perceived black labor exodus. The bureau's concentration on singing the praises of Louisiana sought to attract those who were accustomed to the hard and risky venture of agriculture. The Bureau of Immigration proclaimed, "Now is the time for the enterprising and intelligent races of Europe to secure themselves the cheapest and most comfortable homes in the world, and to acquire quick and certain competence."

Later in 1866, under the subsequent leadership of Dr. Thomas Cottman, the Louisiana Bureau of Immigration noticed:

> *In every part of this state, as soon as you leave the limits of the great plantations during the season of cultivation, we find not only white men, women, and children, boys and girls, laboring at all hours in the fields, without regard to the pretended climatic and miasmatic influences which are so erroneously imagined to be detrimental to white labor…and generally it may be said with equal truth that there is no climate in the world so favorable to the European immigrant than that of Louisiana.*

On February 10, 1869, after three years of research, the Bureau of Immigration issued a report that listed the reasons for aggressive immigration marketing. The bureau's new commissioner, James O. Noyes, was described as "a gentleman of means and enterprise, and a scholar of high and liberal views." Commissioner Noyes composed an elaborate public relations report that related how hesitant immigrants refrained from coming to Louisiana as "the prejudices, passions, hatreds, the false economic theories as to the cultivation of land and the conduct of labor which had outlived the institution of slavery, not only repelled immigration as effectually as slavery had done, but also actually caused an emigration of thousands of our best citizens to the North." Some who ventured to the South found the atmosphere not conducive to successful agriculture and farming, and the volatile political climate contributed to the lack of migrants putting down permanent roots in Louisiana. Other states, such as Missouri, demonstrated success with such missions to attract German émigrés. "It is manifestly our duty," the commissioner declared, "to divest as much as possible of this swelling flood of European immigrants to our shores."

The integral portion of Noyes's assertions had to do with guaranteeing the security and safety of both the persons and property of the immigrants to Louisiana. This would play an important part in Louisiana immigration history, at least when it came to the influx of Italian immigrants who eventually flooded into the region. Commissioner Noyes commented that although there had been previous efforts to entice immigrants to the area— and even though those areas were productive to a point—most immigrants made their way to the interior of the nation. The commissioner reasoned:

As neighborhoods become more thickly settled, poverty gradually disappears. The labor also becomes more severe and more remunerative—less severe because where the population is sparse so much labor has to be directed to maintaining even an imperfect security—more remunerative for the reason that as population becomes more dense and more security is obtained at less cost, more of the products of labor can be saved to be divided between the labor and the capitalist…With the increase of population in a free and progressive State like our own, comes a higher standard of living.

Commissioner Noyes continued with his comments on the prosperity of foreign countries based on the labors of their farmer citizens. Ending poverty resulted from the "diffusion" of various populations from the Old World to the New World, where "as countries grow more prosperous emigration increases. The emigration from a country, except in rare cases, like the exodus which followed the famine in Ireland, is therefore an evidence of prosperity." The advertisement of the advantages of immigrating to Louisiana had to take the forefront in any efforts to attract a new source of labor. "A plain, simple statement of inducements which a State like Louisiana has to offer to immigrants is the very best means to promote immigration," noted Noyes. Louisiana had already established a link with Italy. The fruit trade in the Mediterranean centered on Sicily, and businessmen throughout Louisiana conducted commodities trading with Italy and Sicily. Immigrants who had already settled in the region could be utilized to write letters to their families and friends in the Old Country convincing them to make a better life for their families and their compatriots. Louisiana held the secrets to accomplish these goals.

The central concern for Commissioner Noyes and the success of Italian immigration was transforming the new visitors from Europeans to Americans.

He stated, "We wish to become a homogenous people, speaking the English language, which is fast becoming the language of the civilized world, and adopting those free and liberal institutions which are the strength and pride and glory of the nation." With the expansion of markets overseas and new workers coming to the area, many city and state leaders realized that the new immigrants could increase Louisiana's profitability while satisfying the state's need for agricultural labor.

Later examples of attracting the Mediterranean immigrants to Louisiana took the form of short booklets with titles such as *Louisiana Products, Resources, and Attractions* and *Louisiana and Its Resources: The State of the Future,* in which the Bureau of Immigration tried to leave no stone unturned in conveying the most promising attributes of the state to immigrants seeking a new life in a strange land. "The climate is never too hot or too cold for field work," one booklet proclaimed, and "sunstroke is almost unknown, and ice an inch thick is seldom seen." Refining previous attractions to the state, subsequent brochures lamented, "Cost of living is much lower than in Europe, and with a slight exertion vegetables can be grown all through the year; poultry, with small attention, can be raised for the table; the poorest shot can supply his larder with game."

Because of the success of the public relations campaign, by 1872, Italian immigration caused a great deal of concern among the population of the United States, creating suspicion that some sinister forces might be at work within Italy to "flood" America with poor Italians. Frederick De Luca, consulate general of Italy in the United States, attempted to dispel this belief and, in doing so, championed the position of the immigrants themselves. De Luca stated that research on immigrants entering the country revealed that most of the arrivals needed assistance once they stepped foot on American soil. De Luca cited the Naturalization Act of 1870, which did not discriminate based on the financial means of the immigrants. Criticism from the public precipitated De Luca's response as he sought to disprove various accusations of an Italian conspiracy to deplete Italy of its labor force. Already at this time, even with the shortage of agricultural labor due to the exodus of agrarian workers from southern Italy, De Luca portrayed the Italian government's position as one of conciliatory acceptance. The counsel general opined:

> *Let us suppose that a month ago a telegram had reached New York announcing that by a decree of the Italian government emigration to America had been forbidden. How would the press and public opinion*

*in this country have received the news? Would not the measure have been
denounced as tyrannical and illegal? The American people, who enjoy all
the blessings of freedom, are too generous to wish for its monopoly.*

Not only did De Luca advocate the benevolence of a grateful nation to the
immigrants, but he also championed a determination of the immigrants'
abilities before classifying them as unskilled workers.

The impact of immigrants on the Louisiana economy was an investment
that appeared to succeed, but results took longer than expected. In 1877,
New Orleans newspapers proclaimed a banner year for the region's local
crops. The Annual Review of the Commerce of New Orleans for 1876–
1877 highlighted many cash crops that local economic concerns considered
vital for the post-Reconstruction recovery of Louisiana. Of the crops listed
in the report, sugar seemed the most promising. "It is, therefore, a matter of
general gratification, that, after the destruction of this great interest by the
war—the cane culture has shown a steady, healthy and satisfactory progress,"
the report noted. Predictions for future market success and security in
Louisiana's economic future seemed promising. Interestingly enough, this
report also sang the praises of racial reclamation of Louisiana, stating all
that Louisiana needed was to entice whites from other states. This would
ensure an indigenous exchange for small farmers to sell their crops. Not only
did the report clamor regarding the success of the harvest season, but it also
showed the maturity of the underlying plan of supplementing the state's
white population.

The Louisiana Sugar Planters' Association (LSPA) hoped that the allure
of Louisiana could bring the Italian immigrants to the state's cane fields.
The LSPA investigated the expected arrival of Italians to the area and, in
June 1881, estimated that ships arriving in New Orleans from southern Italy
cost approximately forty dollars per passenger. The association encouraged
this immigration to Louisiana's cane fields based on projected immigrant
arrivals for the next growing season, which spelled success for cane planters.

The Bureau of Immigration not only relied on brochures and
advertisements but also recruited special agents to make sure that those
who desired to travel to the New World but could not afford the journey
received advances to make the trek to America. Unfortunately, this service,
like any other, seethed with corruption and unreliability. The *padrone* system,
or "bossism," originated as a means for the immigrant to pay for his passage
after arriving in the new land by working off the price of that passage.
Descriptions of the *padrone* have characterized him as a "tyrannical person

who hired out his own countrymen, under false business arrangements, to American labor contractors." The *padrone* came to be viewed as an opportunist who preyed on the Italian people wishing to leave Italy and immigrate to the United States. The *padrones* who enlisted men in Italy made claims that they could find the Italians work in America and paid their passage to get there. Although the abundance of workers willing to accept the *padrones'* promises made the trafficking of humans to the United States very profitable, the *padrones* also worked to enlist whole families. This practice enhanced the *padrones'* commission (known as a *bossatura*) and proliferated the use of families in illegal activities once they arrived in America. The men worked in unskilled jobs, the women were often forced into prostitution and the children were forced to shine shoes or steal on the streets. On the one hand, the *padrone* system provided large pools of labor and brought large numbers of these immigrants to the United States. Yet the *padrones* were not trustworthy and gained a reputation for enslaving whole families.

Recognizing that the *padrone* system proved partly beneficial to both immigrants and potential employers, the United States government viewed the system as corrupt and exploitive, and Congress met in session in 1885 to address the issue. In February of that year, Congress passed the Foran Act, which prohibited anyone "to prepay the transportation, or in any way assist or encourage the importations of any alien or aliens, foreigner or foreigners, into the United States, its Territories, or District of Columbia, under contract or agreement, parole or special, express or implied, made previous to the importation or migration to perform such labor or service of any kind in the United States." Even though the Foran Act forbade the boss system from operating legally, it continued clandestinely throughout the "golden era" of Italian immigration of the 1890s.

The arrival of immigrants from overseas garnered media attention and demonstrated the success of the Bureau of Immigration's public relations campaign. "Nearly 1000 of their countrymen are awaiting transportation to this country," one newspaper heralded. Subsequent reports of Italian immigrants arriving in the Crescent City proved very descriptive: "The new arrivals wore the quaint costumes of their native land, and it was apparent that most of them belonged to the peasantry." Still, when boatloads of Italian immigrants arrived from the Mediterranean, people were continually surprised at the appearance of these newcomers. One observer noted, "There was scarcely one of them to whom landing in New Orleans did not mean a reuniting of family ties long severed. There was heartiness about

This photograph shows a man waiting, with others in queue behind him, at the registration desk in the immigration station on Ellis Island; an immigration official is seated at the desk. *Courtesy of the Library of Congress, Prints and Photographs Division.*

their greetings that could not be mistaken for conventional politeness." Most of these arrivals happily greeted family members with kisses and heartfelt emotions for those who "had pioneered for them in this country." These "Sicilians," as characterized through the observations of one eyewitness, "were either fruit growers, or fruit vendors in their native country, and not a few have brought with them small cargoes of Sicilian lemons, while others have included macaroni in their importations."

The media of the day also pointed out that the Italian government, under the direction of then prime minister Francesco Crispi, passed legislation that closely regulated Italian immigration from the southern regions in the mid-1880s and brought the practice under state control. The law provided that "all agents for emigrants to the United States shall give security in the sum of 60,000 francs." Several protests arose against the law, declaring that any Italians wishing to improve their stations in life should be able to freely exercise that privilege. Despite the passage of the Italian law in 1888, immigration to the United States increased.

Once acclimated to their new surroundings, Italian settlements in Louisiana spread into Tangipahoa and St. Tammany Parishes. But New Orleans, by far, constituted the highest concentration of Italians in the state. Italians and Sicilians congregated into the French Quarter section of the city where apartments were dark and cramped and resembled the dinginess of their homeland. Upon arrival, the male immigrants immediately sought employment on the city's docks, unloading the citrus boats arriving daily from South America. Some of the Italians worked as day laborers on the docks of the Mississippi River, while others moved to the more spacious surroundings of cotton and cane country. The immigrants who worked in rural areas of Louisiana often lived in squalid huts on or near the plantation homestead. The Italian women living near the plantation fields cooked and reared children until those children were able to work in the fields alongside their fathers. Because of this work ethic, most of the children had to forego any formal education. The immigrants lived a dismal existence, barely a caste above the slaves who had worked the same fields prior to the emancipation, but they found solace that they were finally in America.

The Louisiana Bureau of Immigration and others like it across the nation served their purpose well. Italians venturing from southern Italy contributed greatly to the growth of the South. During the same time, 1860–80, northern Italians traveled across the Alps into Central Europe, as well as making the journey to South and Latin American destinations to seek their fortunes. Most of the southern Italians took the short junket across the Mediterranean to North Africa, and as the Industrial Revolution began in the United States, Latin and South America suddenly lost their appeal for the Italian immigrant.

STATISTICAL POPULATION FIGURES OF LOUISIANA, 1860–1910

Ethnicity/ Nationality	1860	1870	1880	1890	1900	1910
Italian	897	1,884	2,527	7,772	17,431	20,233
White	277,080	237,453	454,954	558,395	729,612	759,767
Black	18,647	263,956	483,655	559,193	650,804	713,874
Other foreign-born	80,975	61,827	54,146	49,747	59,903	68,389

Although Italian immigration proved beneficial to the South, assessment of the effects of immigration in general caused officials to question whether immigration proved beneficial to the United States. In May 1905, the Southern Industrial Parliament met in Washington, D.C., and discussed the "difficulties involved in the handling of thousands of foreigners annually coming to the United States." Commissioner general of the Bureau of Immigration F.P. Sargent pointed out that an abundance of the immigrants who arrived in the United States remained in the New York area and rarely ventured past the confines of the overcrowded urban areas. Sargent called on the members of the parliament to lobby Congress to establish a visitors' center on Ellis Island to inform new immigrants of the opportunities throughout the country in parts away from the main ports. Sargent anticipated that a multitude of immigrants, Italians included, "would be glad to be directed to the open country, where there is sunshine and plenty of room, and where it would be an advantage to the country to have them located." The commissioner firmly believed in exposing the "alien" to areas outside New York where immigrants might "become good Americans." Many native New Yorkers of the time maintained that the consistent overcrowding of the area would erase any vestige of the original inhabitants, making their history clouded and their heritage even less traceable.

In Louisiana, at the same time as the Southern Industrial Parliament met at the nation's capital, immigration became such a successful venture that further arrivals would make for a labor market that could be dispersed throughout the South, assisting other states in their struggle for economic recovery. Moreover, with such high concentrations of Italians in the state, it became apparent to one observer that "the somewhat unnecessary prejudice which existed for a long time in many southern sections against the importation of foreigners due to causes not necessary to mention here, has been almost obliterated." The reporter made these claims based on the

Immigrants like these pictured made their way to the United States through Ellis Island, where they waited for their approval to join family or friends who were already established with homes and jobs. *Courtesy of the Library of Congress, Prints and Photographs Division.*

prosperity that immigration brought to the businesses of New Orleans and other parishes. However, the "unnecessary prejudice" continued. Italians continued to be stereotyped as part of an underclass judged on their squalid living conditions. Fortunately, hardworking and industrious Italian immigrants who made the journey to Louisiana between 1865 and 1900 would prove to be the backbone of the state's post–Civil War recovery.

The Italians who arrived in Louisiana found that "day labor in industry offers the comfort and companionship of his fellows, usually a home among Italians and the feeling of security and confidence that comes to an ignorant foreigner only when he can make his wants known in his own language." And yet, this would not deter them from trying to break from existing as laborers to becoming landowners. Some succeeded with the transition because Italians saved and opened restaurants, barrooms and grocery stores that proved so successful that they in turn purchased rental property that perpetuated an income not only for themselves but also for their children and, in some cases, their grandchildren. Italian settlements continually grew in America and in the South, both in rural and urban areas. This provided

Johnnie is a nine-year-old oyster shucker. The man with the pipe is a *padrone* who had brought these people from Baltimore for four years. He said, "I tell you I have to lie to 'em. Ther're never satisfied. Hard work to get them." He is the boss of the shucking shed in Dunbar, Louisiana, 1900. Courtesy *of the Library of Congress, Prints and Photographs Division.*

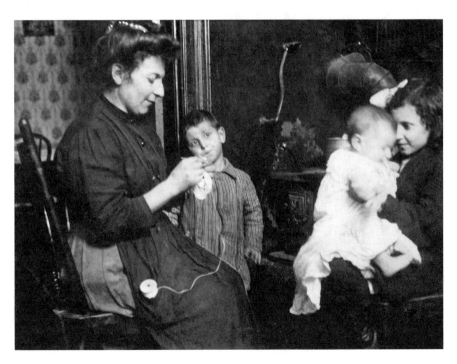

An Italian family in an immigrant tenement, 1910. *Courtesy of the Library of Congress, Prints and Photographs Division.*

for newer immigrants to become better acclimated to their new surroundings more easily, joining their fellow compatriots in settlements that continued to grow. Italians adjusted well to their new environment but did not share in their hosts' disdain for blacks.

In the wake of a nationalist revolution at home in Italy, southern Italians saw their lifestyles worsen instead of improve. Seeing an opportunity to elevate themselves economically and help with the economic recovery of Louisiana, they made their way to an amiable climate and pursued the occupations of their ancestors, forging ahead with a new life. However beneficial their settlement in Louisiana may have been for those concerned, Italians were unfamiliar with southern racial mores. Often disoriented with their place in society, the years of feeling unequal to their northern Italian neighbors contributed to southern Italians' feelings of social inadequacy in Louisiana.

By the early part of the twentieth century, Italians in Louisiana had worked hard to establish themselves in businesses and occupations that not only contributed to the economic success of the region but also provided professional foundations for their descendants. In working to create these foundations and becoming successful in a majority of instances, the Italians of Louisiana would suffer the indignities of discrimination and prejudice.

Chapter 2

The Influence of Nativism

Hyphenated Americans…have poured the poison of disloyalty into the very arteries of our national life…such creatures of passion, disloyalty and anarchy must be crushed out!
—President Woodrow Wilson, 1915

America offered the new Italian immigrant freedom, yet "native" Americans subsequently sought to limit or restrict that freedom. Once the level of immigration reached a point considered critical mass, American citizens became agitated at the overcrowding of cities and jobs being taken away from Americans; they considered the immigrants harbingers of disease and users of the stiletto dagger (hence the "dago" moniker). Americans—who forgot that their roots in this country began with the immigration of their ancestors—began to despise the Italians and adopted that hatred and racism as canons.

Anti-foreign sentiment began in earnest in the 1850s as the Whig Party disintegrated. These nativists made sporadic protestations concerning immigrants in the 1830s. Not only did the anti-foreign movement reject welcoming immigrants to the United States, but it also rejected Roman Catholicism from the Holy See in Rome that allegedly ruled over a vast worldly empire that included citizens of various nations. This sentiment grew to a fever pitch as the new American Party, or Know-Nothings, learned that burning churches, homes and convents and provoking violence against the Irish, Germans and, eventually, blacks proved detrimental to any serious political movement to eliminate foreigners from American shores.

A bust portrait of a young man representing the nativist ideal of the Know-Nothing Party. He wears a bold tie and a fedora-type hat tilted at a rakish angle. *Courtesy of the Library of Congress, Prints and Photographs Division.*

The Know-Nothing Party incited the paranoia of the public in capitalizing on Americans' alarm at the waves of immigrants arriving in the United States toward the end of the 1840s. In the 1850s, the Know-Nothings saw their popularity gain momentum, especially in Louisiana, where, in 1853, cholera and yellow fever epidemics devastated the New Orleans population.

Know-Nothings within the state blamed newly arrived immigrants for the spread of the diseases. They incited their listeners with vitriol that stereotyped immigrants such as the Irish, who supposedly fought among themselves, drank heavily and existed in rather deplorable conditions. This stereotype provided some credibility to the Know-Nothing rhetoric. With the number of immigrants arriving daily in Louisiana through New Orleans from ports all over the world and the incessant overcrowding of different parts of the city (Italians in the Vieux Carré and the Irish in the uptown area), the Know-Nothings found little difficulty in convincing the citizens of New Orleans of the inevitability of a foreign invasion—an invasion that threatened not only the economic survival of the nation but also the health and welfare of the area's inhabitants.

The district attorney's race for the Parish of Orleans in 1853 demonstrated the lengths to which the Know-Nothings went to ensure the preservation of native Americanism, as well as cajole the populace into becoming their supporters in a perceived battle with the foreigners. E.J. Carroll, an Irishman, ran for the office. The Know-Nothings proclaimed, "Mr. Carroll is a Roman Catholic, a bigot: all his family are Catholics…Americans! Shall we be ruled by Irish and Germans?" Know-Nothings preyed on the citizens' consternation with the dangerous prediction that, should Carroll be elected, "he would discharge every person brought before the Criminal Court, provided he is a creole [*sic*] of Ireland or Germany." Carroll responded that he depended on the voters to elect him, no matter their religion or country of origin, and he attempted to allay any trepidation on the part of New Orleans citizenry when he stated, "I presume people will (as they should) vote according to the current of their feelings and the dictates of their judgment." Carroll's plea went unheeded, and he was handily defeated by B.S. Tappan. The Know-Nothings' influence intensified with virility.

"Is it fit that a populous and a strong nation, on its own soil, be governed by a comparative handful of foreigners," a Know-Nothing editorial queried, "ignorant of its laws yet claiming to administer them, and seizing upon its offices while yet hardly speaking its language?" The alleged "outrage" of immigrant invasions and the protestations of foreigners seeking elected office culminated in fighting and riots between the Know-Nothings and immigrants in New Orleans. The American Party of Louisiana called for American citizens to "take the field at once and better ourselves like those who stood at Waterloo."

During southern political campaigns during the latter part of the 1850s, local politicians vehemently contested one another's records, especially on the issue of slavery. Know-Nothings used this political powder keg to their advantage, arguing that "immigrants to the southern states opposed slavery because they competed with slave labor and because they came from countries where slavery did not exist." Because most immigrants had settled in the North, populations there rose dramatically, therefore giving the "North's majority over the South in Congress."

The Know-Nothings' platform could not sustain itself for long, and their decline, especially in the South, came rapidly between 1856 and 1861. In the presidential election of 1856, the Know-Nothing candidate, Millard Fillmore, ran third. Furthermore, the party stood divided over the issue of slavery, and even though it attempted to coerce the populace into an anti-foreigner frenzy, this ideology did not appeal to most of the Catholic citizens of Louisiana. Although some elements of the Know-Nothings remained in the state after the party's official decline, the arrival of Admiral David G. Farragut in May 1862 signified the end of the American Party. Yet the echoes of anti-foreignism and white supremacy rang out during Reconstruction.

The Know-Nothing Party laid the foundation for a rebirth of ethnic hatred in southern Louisiana. The Irish and German populations suffered the most from this movement, but eventually Italians and blacks in the southern part of the state felt the sting of nativism. The fear the Know-Nothings generated had nothing to do with racial and ethnic verbosity; rather, it reflected a stereotype associated with Italians themselves. The lack of prejudices Italians exhibited made them prime targets for any nativist condemnation.

With the end of the Civil War and the beginning of Reconstruction in the South, the enmity against the Italians slowly matured until whites who believed the nativist agenda recognized an opportunity to demonize Italians. Whites then resorted to murder in demonstrating their conviction to a return to antebellum racial boundaries. Throughout this whole period, the Italians' diligence to become Americans never wavered as events affecting their future unfolded around them.

Chapter 3

A Catalyst to Violence

His life was honorable and Brave; His fidelity to duty was sealed with his death.
—*epitaph on the tomb of David C. Hennessy*

As the Italians worked to further themselves and their families, the threat of nativism seemed a passing fancy that would end with the movement's demise. Unfortunately, that threat would become deeply rooted in the minds of whites in Louisiana. White supremacy had become permanently entrenched within the framework of state politics, culture and everyday life. The Italians, for the most part, had nothing to fear at this time, as most of the aggression and prejudice was directed toward the black population of the state, but soon their situation changed. In fact, the Italians survived Reconstruction relatively unscathed, but in the fall of 1890, with the commission of one crime in particular, the Italian population of Louisiana would face a maddened hatred never before seen in the South.

This malevolence against Italians began at 11:00 p.m. on the drizzly night of October 15, 1890. After a late dinner of oysters and milk with a friend and fellow New Orleans police officer, thirty-four-year-old Chief David C. Hennessy walked to his home down Girod Street to the residence he shared with his elderly mother. The sidewalks on Girod Street where the chief lived were muddy from the incessant drizzling, and he decided to take a post-dinner stroll. Leaving his dinner companion, William J. O'Connor, two blocks from his house, Chief Hennessy arrived at 275 Girod Street, walked onto his porch, unlocked his front door and, before opening it, turned his head slightly when he heard some whispers coming from the street. As he turned his whole body toward the sounds, shotgun blasts and smoke permeated the air. Large, hot pellets seared through the chief's topcoat and vest. Slugs tore into his abdomen and intestines, while other buckshot broke his right elbow and another pellet burrowed into his right leg. The rest of his clothes were peppered with smaller shot. The chief reached for his service revolver and tried to return fire, but because of his wounds, he managed to fire only four inaccurate shots. Hennessy dropped to his knees.

Police Officer J.C. Roe, who walked a beat through Hennessy's neighborhood at approximately the same time every evening, made his way to the sounds of the gunfire and encountered the gunmen during the mêlée. Officer Roe drew his weapon, but before he could find cover and return fire, a bullet grazed his left ear, and when he tried firing his weapon, it jammed. He retreated. Hennessy, with great effort and in excruciating pain, recovered to his feet and staggered around the corner to the residence of Mr. Henry Gillis at 189 Basin Street, where he collapsed on the porch.

In O'Connor's eyewitness account of the night of the shooting, he stated that he left the chief, walked about a block and then heard the shotgun blasts. O'Connor ran back to Hennessy's residence after hearing the report and found a trail of blood leading from Hennessy's front door to Gillis's front porch. O'Connor knelt down to the side of his friend and asked Hennessy if he knew who shot him. "Oh Billy, Billy, they have given it to me and I gave them back the best way I could," Hennessy responded under labored breathing. O'Connor then asked, "Who gave it to you, Dave?" Hennessy motioned O'Connor to place his ear near Hennessy's mouth, where he whispered, "The dagoes." Police Sergeant Richard Walsh later asked Hennessy specifically who shot him. Hennessy "shook his head from side to side in a negative way."

An ambulance rushed Chief Hennessy to Charity Hospital, where doctors examined the wounds he had received from the shotgun blasts to the chest and stomach area and deemed them fatal. The doctors could not control the bleeding, and the chief's friends gathered near his bedside could only wait. At 8:00 p.m. the next evening, October 16, 1890, Reverend Father O'Neill performed the last rites on Chief Hennessy. As his mother stood by his side, witnesses heard Hennessy mutter, "Mother, what do you want down here? I'll be home by and by." After his assurance, Hennessy fell asleep and breathed easily. At 9:20 p.m., he succumbed to his wounds and expired. In a subsequent autopsy report, assistant Orleans Parish coroner H.J. Scherch found that "death was caused by internal hemorrhage, the result of a wound situated three inches below the nipple in the left axillary line." This wound, of all the others, proved the most fatal, as the slugs passed through both lungs.

Chief Hennessy's body lay in state at his residence on Girod Street from 4:00 p.m. on October 17 until 10:00 a.m. the next day. An elegant hearse then transported the body to Gallier Hall, the city's administrative building. One observer noted, "All day long the people crowded in to view the body and it was almost impossible to reach the bier, which had been placed in the same room in which the body of Jefferson Davis lay in state...The cortege moved through the principle streets of the city, all of which were so crowded with people as to blockade the street cars and the passage of vehicles." A police honor guard escorted the body from the old city hall on St. Charles Avenue, where mourners visited the fallen chief for four more hours. Father O'Neill, the same cleric who had issued the last rites at Charity Hospital, officiated at the service. At 3:00 p.m., twenty-one pallbearers loaded the coffin onto a hearse and escorted the cortege to St. Joseph's Church on Tulane Avenue. Crowds blocked the streets so that streetcars and other horse-drawn vehicles could not pass. Hennessy's remains were laid to rest at the Metairie Cemetery on the corner of Metairie Road and City Park Avenue. Prominent citizens of the city of New Orleans solicited funds for and subsequently erected a monument to Hennessy's spirit as the revered crime fighter.

Chief Hennessy became the quintessential hero of the New Orleans masses in their perceived fight against a foreign underworld conspiracy that threatened to terrorize the city's law-abiding citizens. Portrayed as a selfless champion by his benefactors, various historical accounts depict a man accustomed to living with violence. Hennessy's rise to the top executive position of the New Orleans Police Department contained many instances of arrogance and bravado filled with confrontation at every turn. Examination of Hennessy's propensity to use violence reflected his upbringing and his father's reputation for solving problems with unprovoked brutality. This leads one to conclude that the young Hennessy grew up knowing the value of violence and recognizing its use for achieving respect in and exacting fear from suspects.

Hennessy's father, Dave, was a member of the Union force under the command of Major General Benjamin F. Butler that invaded and occupied the city of New Orleans in May 1862. The elder Hennessy, by all accounts, took his role as an "oppressor" seriously. After completing his term of enlistment with the Union army, Dave joined the Metropolitans, a quasi-police force used by the Radical Republican governors during the

The tomb of Police Chief David C. Hennessy. The monument was paid for by several prominent citizens of the city. Metairie Cemetery, New Orleans, Louisiana. *Courtesy of the author.*

Reconstruction period that enlisted the help of former African American members of the occupying Union army to populate the force.

David C. Hennessy was born in 1858. In 1867, when young David was only nine years old, Dave Hennessy became involved in a barroom brawl that escalated into a gunfight. The elder Hennessy died of gunshot wounds sustained in the brawl, leaving his wife and son to survive in a hostile southern environment. After the death of her husband, Hennessy's mother approached the chief of the Metropolitans, General Algernon Badger, to put young David to work. Out of a sense of loyalty to the elder Hennessy, General Badger employed David as a messenger for his office. This began David's career in law enforcement, and he rose steadily through the ranks. At seventeen, Hennessy joined the police force as a patrol officer. When former Confederate hero Francis T. Nicholls won the governor's election in 1876, he disbanded the Metropolitans and replaced them with the Boylan Detective Agency under the direction of Colonel Thomas N. Boylan.

The Metropolitans gained a reputation as storm troopers for Radical Reconstruction in Louisiana. Colonel Thomas N. Boylan absorbed some of the former Metropolitan force into his own agency. Colonel Boylan enlisted the young Hennessy as a detective with his agency, and the young firebrand made his reputation in this atmosphere as power struggles within law enforcement and city government evolved into vicious and sometimes deadly competitions.

In 1881, Boylan engaged Detective Hennessy to track and eventually apprehend one of the most violent and elusive Italian bandits of the late nineteenth century, Giuseppe Esposito. Esposito hailed from Palermo, Sicily, where the inhabitants considered him to be the most dangerous *bandito* in Sicilian history. At the height of his ascendancy, this "brigand prince" came to the attention of the "King of the Brigands," a mysterious character known only as Leone. After they met for the first time, Esposito became one of Leone's top lieutenants, steadily rising to second in command of the brigand band. The brigands in Sicily made their fortunes through kidnapping and extortion, and one much-publicized case involved Esposito and subsequently caused his flight from the island. John Forster Rose, an English adventurer, was hiking in the hills of Sicily when Esposito and his band saw an opportunity to hold Rose for ransom. Rose's wife soon received a letter sent to the couple's London home demanding £5,000. Three more letters subsequently arrived; the final two contained one of Rose's ears in each. Mrs. Rose paid the ransom after the fourth letter. Esposito returned Rose to England, and the British government demanded satisfaction. Italian authorities suppressed the brigandage in Sicily, but Esposito fled to America.

In the spring of 1881, a newspaper reporter walked along Customhouse Street in New Orleans enjoying a beautiful sunny southern day. He observed a small, stocky-looking man gesturing wildly toward a young Italian woman standing in front of a small restaurant. The woman seemed equally agitated, waving her hands with rage at every word the man said. Finally, after a few moments of witnessing this argument, the reporter heard the young woman yell, "*Bandito!*" and saw her hurl a soda bottle at the man's head. The man grabbed the woman suddenly and drew her closer to him. Seeing that the episode might escalate, the reporter approached the couple. The man released the young woman and smiled at the reporter. He said in broken English, "What can you do with-a those-a woman?"

The reporter unknowingly spoke with Esposito, the *bandito*, although by March 1881, the Italian population in New Orleans knew the stranger as

Randazzo. Randazzo married a woman with two children and changed his name in order to avoid detection. Under pressure from the British government, the Italian government hired two New York detectives, James Mooney and D. Boland, to track and possibly capture the elusive criminal. Detectives Mooney and Boland followed Esposito from New York to New Orleans and confirmed their target through two New Orleans detectives: Mike Hennessy and his cousin, David C. Hennessy. On July 5, 1881, the four men shadowed and then surrounded the suspect with revolvers drawn. Following his capture, the State of New York extradited the man claiming to be Randazzo for a hearing to determine his return to the jurisdiction of Italian authorities. After his arrest, the suspect produced papers identifying himself as "Vincent Rebello." On September 14, 1881, the United States commissioner present at the extradition hearing confirmed the identity of the suspect as that of Giuseppe Esposito, the man wanted in Sicily for the kidnapping and mutilation of John Forster Rose, as well as other brigandage crimes. Executing the warrant for extradition, Esposito returned to Italy, where he served out his life in prison.

Except for a few Italians living in the area, no one knew Esposito was in New Orleans. His capture occurred because of business dealings: Esposito had a disagreement with another Sicilian immigrant, Tony Labousse (or Labuzzo), who oversaw the construction of a boat Esposito commissioned. Labousse delivered the boat in time, but Esposito reneged on payment and Labousse sought his revenge by revealing the bandit's true identity to the police. Labousse never received the reward placed on Esposito's head by the Italian government because shortly after the arrest, one of Esposito's associates allegedly shot and killed Labousse.

When Hennessy returned to New Orleans from New York, the citizenry of New Orleans hailed him as a crime-fighting hero and the number one nemesis of the Italian underworld. With the successful capture and extradition of Esposito, Hennessy's value to the law enforcement community grew, as well as his thirst for power within that venue. Confidence in his abilities as a detective grew, and Hennessy saw an opportunity to achieve a milestone at his young age (he was twenty-three at the time of Esposito's capture): chief of detectives. However, the political climate in New Orleans in the 1880s created an enemy who almost cost Hennessy his career. A feud erupted as a result of Mike Hennessy's aspirations to a higher position within the Boylan Agency. The Hennessys' war with Thomas Devereaux became a much-publicized affair and demonstrated the sometimes bloody personal feuding involved in politics in nineteenth-century New Orleans.

Thomas Devereaux emerges from New Orleans history as a character who makes a historian wonder how he lived so long. Devereaux walked the fine line between criminal and public servant. In 1881, as a member of the New Orleans City Council, Devereaux proposed a police board in an attempt to rid the city of its much-publicized corruption. The reorganization of the police did "not involve necessarily the removal of any member of the existing force; but such measures might be adopted as would necessitate the removal of certain members, or even a change in the personnel of the whole body of police." The police board succeeded briefly; several officers saw their law enforcement careers either suspended or ended. Actions of the new body appeared in the local newspaper and appeared to serve the public good. A local newspaper reported, "Officer O'Roarke, having been found asleep on his beat, was fined two days' pay...Officer C. Wolfe, for drunkenness, was dismissed the force, and Officer J. Melia was docked one days' pay." The police board would figure substantially in the promotion of officers as well and served as a tool for those in charge to eliminate officers they deemed politically undesirable. This created more volatility in the politically charged atmosphere of the city.

The New Orleans City Council appointed Devereaux as the "chief of aids," responsible for all police detectives. A political appointee with a questionable pedigree, Devereaux hardly earned the respect of a city known for its corrupt police force and rampant crime. One incident of particular note occurred in February 1876. A former New Orleans detective, Robert Harris, was standing on a street corner when "a man in a light-colored suit put a bullet in the back of his head" and casually walked away. Police suspected Devereaux to be the shooter and knew he carried concealed weapons, but when police searched him later as he lurked near the crime scene, they found no firearms. Devereaux was taken in for questioning, but police later released him.

Devereaux helped fuel his own mercurial reputation by publicizing his feuds with the city council, and especially other officers and Mayor Shakspeare, in local newspapers. Colonel Boylan believed Devereaux incapable of cleaning up the detective bureau and believed he would also rid the bureau of Boylan's appointees. Two of these appointees included Mike and David Hennessy. Devereaux's career began to lapse when he tried to use his office to fulfill Boylan's prophecy. Mike and David Hennessy would not only be the end of Devereaux's career but also the instruments of his demise.

The first incident that spelled Devereaux's decline came when he attempted to charge Mike Hennessy with drunkenness on duty, assaulting a citizen and dereliction of duty by frequenting a bordello while at his post. Devereaux also charged David Hennessy with being absent from his post. On October 30,

1881, a police board of review examined the charges against the two detectives, along with evidence to the contrary of Devereaux's assertions. Devereaux even went so far as to plant a news story predetermining Mike's guilt. Even though the police review board acquitted Mike and David Hennessy of any malfeasance in office, the two held Devereaux in lower regard than before the debacle and vowed revenge against the city council's champion.

On October 31, 1881, Devereaux met with John W. Fairfax at the latter's brokerage offices on Gravier Street to discuss some of his business dealings. Outside the St. Charles Avenue side of the office window, Mike Hennessy suddenly appeared, brandishing a revolver. Mike opened fire and broke the windows on both sides of the office. Devereaux returned fire at Mike, hitting him in the neck, with the bullet exiting through his jaw and mouth. As Devereaux aimed to fire again at Mike, David appeared from behind him and fired point blank into the back of Devereaux's head, killing him instantly. Instead of waiting for the police to arrive, David helped Mike to his feet and brought his wounded cousin to Charity Hospital. Police later arrested Mike and David for the murder of Thomas Devereaux.

At the trial of Mike and David Hennessy, witnesses testified about the actions of the defendants on the day of the murder, and it appeared to anyone in the courtroom that day to be a case of vengeful, premeditated murder. Defense attorneys Lionel Adams and A.J. Henriques put the victim on trial, often comparing Hennessy's "reputation for good and quietness" with Devereaux's "dangerous disposition." The prosecution offered testimony to rebut the defense's characterization of the victim, but their offerings did not sway the jury. Mike and David Hennessy were acquitted of Devereaux's murder.

Even though the jury vindicated Mike and David Hennessy, the two former detectives found it difficult to find gainful employment subsequent to their trial. Mike moved to Houston and a few years later died from gunshot wounds he received during a mysterious ambush where the assailant (or assailants) escaped without identification. David found employment as a bank detective with the Farrell Detective Agency, and as a special detective with A.J. Farrell's agency, he distinguished himself through various assignments, including as chief of security for the 1884 Cotton Centennial Exposition held in New Orleans. Farrell died shortly after the Cotton Exposition, so Hennessy partnered with his former employer, Thomas Boylan.

In 1888, after a hiatus of six years from the political limelight, Joseph A. Shakspeare, who served as mayor of New Orleans from 1880 to 1882, ran again for the office and won under a reform ticket. By this time, the New Orleans Police Department had run rampant with corruption and graft.

Remembering the young man once hailed as the crime-fighting hero of New Orleans, Mayor Shakspeare appointed David Hennessy to the post of superintendent of police of the city of New Orleans. Shakspeare hoped the political climate had changed enough for him to implement true reforms in his new term, with one of those endeavors being his "intent upon taking up the fight once again to capture the Police Department."

With Hennessy's appointment as superintendent of police in 1888, the city believed an era of reform was forthcoming with the police force. Despite Hennessy's rough rapport, the reputation of a "good and quiet disposition" that had acquitted him in the Devereaux trial raised the expectations of those who were tired of a corrupt and ineffective police force. Within the first three weeks of his administration, Chief Hennessy fired forty-two officers for dereliction of duty. Chief Hennessy also tightened the police force application process by implementing educational requirements, and to add a sense of pride and honor, he furnished his officers with new uniforms and paid them higher salaries. Moreover, Mayor Shakspeare proposed a new law that closed all gambling houses in an attempt to reduce the temptation of graft among patrolmen. The law went into effect on October 3, 1888.

Hennessy saw himself in his new position as a mediator between the warring factions of the alleged Italian crime organizations of the city. The chief made a study of the reputed "families" in the area and sacrificed impartiality by becoming involved in one dispute that some historians have attributed to his death. The Provenzano and Matranga factions fought for control of the New Orleans docks from 1888 to 1890 as the lucrative fruit importation business grew, expanding the New Orleans economy and creating an avenue for alleged aggressive underworld figures to make money illegally through graft and extortion. The Matrangas became the victims of a turf war that ultimately involved Chief Hennessy in which certain underworld factions would align against him for his involvement.

Charles and Antonio Matranga, together with Italian businessman Joseph Macheca, convinced stevedores and dockworkers to work for their fruit importing concerns, even though the Provenzano family already employed these workers. The Matranga/Macheca faction established a monopoly over the docks, and rumors whispered in underworld circles stated that the Matrangas declared war against the other rival families, specifically the Provenzanos. Chief Hennessy tried to smooth things between the two families, but this only fueled rumors that the police department had reverted to its corrupt ways and that Chief Hennessy solicited bribes for protection of the Provenzanos.

On May 5, 1890, after a long day of emptying a large steamer named the *Foxhall*, dockworkers Gerolamo "Jim" Caruso, Salvatore Sunzeri, Antonio "Tony" Matranga, Sebastiano Incardona, Tony and Frank Locascio and Vincent Caruso (Jim's brother and Matranga and Locascio foreman) piled into Matranga's wagon for a ride to their respective homes. Lumbering toward the French Quarter, Jim Caruso exited the wagon, bidding the other riders goodnight, and entered his home. As the wagon reached the corner of Ursuline and Dorgenois Streets, one of the men began to sing in Italian, and despite their exhausted conditions, the others joined in. The men finally made it to their homes as they approached the intersection of Claiborne and Esplanade. Incardona noticed six men at the corner whom he surmised stood there waiting for a streetcar. The waiting men yelled something in Italian and then raised shotguns and fired at the wagon. Tony Matranga took some buckshot to the right thigh, but Incardona remained unharmed as he dove under the wagon's front seat to avoid the barrage. The incident took only a few seconds, and Matranga was the lone casualty. Later that same day, Jim and Vincent Caruso, Sunzeri, Matranga, Incardona and the Locascios identified Joseph and Peter Provenzano, Tony Pellegrini, Nick Guillio, Tony Gianforcaro and Gaspardo Lombardo as the men who fired on their wagon. The Provenzano-Matranga struggle for control of the docks bubbled to the surface and led many New Orleanians to suspect a blood feud had been executed that May evening. At first, it appeared that the Provenzanos' arrest signified a stand against the seething criminal element, but opponents of Mayor Shakspeare and Chief Hennessy saw the ambush and the subsequent arrests of the identified suspects as Hennessy's way of demonstrating his power over the Provenzanos.

A few months later, the Provenzanos' trial took place, but because of a technicality, Judge Joshua Baker granted the convicted men a new trial set for October 22, 1890. The Matrangas were angered that a new trial had been granted, and the "family" began to think that Chief Hennessy had played a part in getting the retrial granted. Additionally, rumors circulated that Hennessy would testify at the trial himself, exposing all the secrets about the criminal underworld he had learned through his attempts to secure a truce between the two factions.

But Hennessy would not get the chance to testify at the Provenzano trial.

Scarcely five hours after Hennessy's death, Mayor Shakspeare made an impassioned speech in front of the New Orleans City Council. Shakspeare expressed his "grief at the loss of a true friend and efficient officer… indignation that he should have died at the hands of assassins…the circumstances of the cowardly deed. We owe it to ourselves and to everything

Inscription on the tomb. *Courtesy of the author.*

we hold sacred in this life to see to it that this blow is the last. We must teach these people a lesson that they will not forget for all time." Mayor Shakspeare further implored that no community throughout the United States existed without "murder societies in its midst. The Sicilian who immigrated to the United States must relinquish any desire for vendetta, and rely on the laws of the United States to remedy any injustice."

Hennessy's well-documented no-nonsense style earned him a reputation that supposedly angered many in underworld circles, and police looked to those circles for their suspects in his murder. An unprecedented roundup of suspects began in the city, as well as "nocturnal visits in domiciles of peaceable Italians." Police detained forty-two suspects on suspicion of committing the act, but many secured release as police narrowed down the field. After an extensive interrogation process, police arrested nineteen suspects for their alleged complicity in the murder of Chief Hennessy, including Pietro Natali, Antonio Scaffedi, Antonio Bagnetto, Manuel Polizzi, Antonio Marchese, Pietro Monasterio, Sebastiano Incardona, Salvador Sunzeri, Loretto Comitez, Carlo Traina and Charles Politz. Law enforcement officials believed the Matrangas sought their revenge for Hennessy's "alliance" with the Provenzanos. Joseph Macheca, a well-known fruit importer, turned himself in to authorities when he learned the district attorney had issued a warrant for his arrest.

After the arrests of the Italians and Macheca's surrender, anti-Italian sentiment rose all over the city of New Orleans. On October 17, 1890, Thomas Duffy, a young newsboy, walked to the Old Orleans Parish Prison on Treme Street and convinced the guards near the front gate that he could positively identify one of the prisoners as one of the men who killed Chief

Hennessy. Guards brought suspect Antonio Scaffedi to the gate, where Duffy could get a better look at the prisoner. Without warning, Duffy brandished a pistol from underneath his shirt and shot Scaffedi in the neck. Arrested and charged with "shooting with intent to kill and wounding less than mayhem," Duffy later sought leniency with the court by pleading insanity. As one person later observed, Duffy "was generally regarded as slightly demented." Duffy stated he suffered from extreme grief over Chief Hennessy's death.

Italians all over the nation exhibited fear with the arrest of the men suspected in Chief Hennessy's murder, and some even felt the unsafe cloud that hung over the city and fled, going back to Italy. A national news service article appeared on October 19, 1890, proclaiming that New Orleans readied itself for a great social disorder and "it seems certain that the city is on the eve of a bloody race riot." Unsubstantiated rumors quickly spread that the accused men waiting in the Orleans Parish Prison also planned to "kill a number of other officials." Public sentiment against all Italians in New Orleans rose alarmingly.

Even though the suspicions of an alleged criminal conspiracy loomed heavily over the nineteen inmates in the Orleans Parish Prison on Treme Street, others speculated about another, more sinister, plot for Hennessy's demise. An editorialist opined:

> There are many who never did believe that the dagoes murdered Chief Hennessy for their own account, or for their satisfaction if he really was murdered by dagoes, and so generally was this theory shared…The question arose as to whether or not others than dagoes might have been associated with the murder. Some attention to this important suggestion has resulted in connecting several prominent men with the plot to assassinate the police superintendent. No disclosure will be made for the present, but it is hoped within the next twenty-four hours the astonishing fact will be made public. If the information herein referred to prove true, then New Orleans has indeed struck a horrible era.

With the perceived threat against the lives of other New Orleans politicos and feeling a self-righteous duty to expose secret societies within the city, on October 18, 1890, Mayor Shakspeare formed a Committee of the Fifty to "devise necessary means and effectual and speedy measures for uprooting and total annihilation of such hell-born associations." Chaired by Edgar H. Ferrar and later Walter C. Flowers, two prominent businessmen within the city, the Committee of the Fifty, which consisted of the city's economic and political elite, resolved to not only root out these "oath-bound assassins" but also to "prevent the introduction here of criminals or paupers from Europe." The committee met regularly, in secret, for the next six months and stated that it intended to "put an end peacefully and lawfully if we can, *violently and summarily* if we must," to rid the city of secret societies.

By October 21, 1890, news of the arrests reached the highest corridors of state and national governments, as well as Italian dignitaries in Washington, D.C. James G. Blaine, secretary of state under President Benjamin Harrison, expressed concern to Governor Nicholls about the nationality of the incarcerated prisoners:

> *The Italian minister represents that, according to advices from the Italian counsel in New Orleans, the mayor in that city caused arrests of innocent persons and issued proclamations tending to incite the entire Italian colony. The minister is confident that the great body of Italians repudiates with horror the acts of a few criminals, and have no desire than to see the law take its course and punish the murderers of the chief of police.*

Governor Nicholls simply replied, "I do not apprehend any trouble."

Officials in Rome became nervous, exchanging frantic reports between their office, the Italian ambassador to the United States, Baron Saverio Fava, and the Italian consul in New Orleans, Pascale Corté. Corté stated in a letter dated November 13, 1890, to a grand jury investigating the prison that some of the inmates there confided in Consul Corté when he visited them. Pietro Natale gave a yard captain some extortion money and suffered a beating at the guards' hands despite the payment. Sebastiano Incardona and Antonio Marchese both stated to Corté that guards beat them repeatedly and had stolen their valuables upon their arrival at the prison. Pietro Monasterio leveled a more serious accusation against the guards when he stated that "he had been beaten and showed several wounds on his head; furthermore he asserted that being ill, on several occasions he asked for a physician, but none appeared."

Baron Fava received a copy of Corté's letter and expressed deep concern over the inmates' accusations; but more importantly, Fava questioned the legality of imprisoning some of the Italians in the first place, as they may be considered Italian citizens. Being an experienced diplomat who had represented his country's interests throughout many parts of the world, Fava used that experience to discover whether any of the incarcerated Italians received unfavorable treatment. Fava wrote to Secretary Blaine, in very diplomatic and courteous language, "The Italian counsel in New

Orleans has referred to me that, information reached him of ill treatments and extortions undergone by several Italian subjects who were arrested in connection with the atrocious murder perpetuated on the chief of police." Blaine subsequently forwarded Fava's correspondence to Governor Nicholls. The governor replied, "An investigation has taken place, resulting in the bringing of indictments against two persons for various acts of brutality against prisoners in parish prison." Governor Nicholls assured Secretary Blaine that those two indictees would receive their due justice. Moreover, the state's chief executive maintained that the system in the prison for which two people were indicted, extortion and physical abuse, existed long before the Italians arrived there, and their nationality had nothing to do with their abuse. Governor Nicholls never identified the two indicted individuals.

While the debate continued concerning the treatment of the Italian prisoners and the eventual Italian government involvement, on November 9, 1890, the district attorney for Orleans Parish, C.H. Luzenberg, convened a grand jury to consider evidence against the accused killers. The grand jury returned indictments against eleven of the accused for murder, plus eight others for accessories after the fact.

On January 21, 1891, the Provenzanos and their alleged accomplices stood trial for the Matranga ambush. Defense attorneys produced witnesses who testified that the accused men were not in the vicinity at the time of the attack. A Sergeant Cooper had stood duty outside the Eden Theater near Customhouse and Royal Street. Cooper remembered seeing two men resembling Tony Provenzano and Nick Guillio in one of the upper floors of the theater on the night of the ambush. Corroboration of Cooper's testimony came from the Third District's Corporal Gabe Porteous, who stated he "saw Provenzano in the Eden Theater the same time Cooper did," although he could not remember seeing Joseph Provenzano, Tony Pellegrini, Nick Guillio, Tony Gianforcaro or Garpardo Lombardo. On January 23, 1891, a jury acquitted the accused of all charges.

To defend the accused men of the murder of Chief Hennessy, Charles Matranga and Joseph Macheca, both wealthy shipping magnates by period standards, hired Lionel Adams, a partner in the firm of Adams & O'Malley. Adams had gained a reputation in the South as a "crack trial lawyer." The accused also hired A.J. Henriques, a former prosecutor with Orleans Parish, who also had a reputation as an outstanding legal mind, and Thomas J. Semmes, attorney and jurisprudence scholar. Along with the legal assistance, the defense utilized the talents of a resourceful and effective private investigator, Dominick J. O'Malley, who was Lionel Adams's partner.

For the prosecution, District Attorney of Orleans Parish C.H. Luzenberg represented the people of Louisiana.

Adams, Henriques, O'Malley and Semmes realized the uphill battle they faced: the prejudices of a major metropolitan city's population, the incorrect characterization of the martyred chief and the mystique of underworld criminal involvement spelled difficulty in achieving an acquittal. Sequestering jurors was not a common practice in Louisiana, however, and the nativist reporting of the local papers presented further difficulties for a fair trial.

The first indication that New Orleans's legal system would prosecute this trial more intensely than other trials came with a minor plea from the defense. Charles Matranga asked from his jail cell at the Orleans Parish Prison to speak with a private investigator and a reporter. Orleans Parish sheriff Gabriel Villeré refused Matranga's request. Attorney Adams filed for a mandamus proceeding on Matranga's behalf in an attempt to force the sheriff to comply with Matranga's appeal. Judge Robert Marr refused to hear the mandamus motion, forcing Adams to seek relief for his client in a higher court. When the State Court of Appeals refused to overturn Judge Marr's decision, Adams appealed to the State Supreme Court. The Supreme Court reviewed the appeal and stated that Sheriff Villeré claimed "he had, in such matters, a discretion which the court could not control." The Supreme Court, in its review, refused to make a concrete decision and asserted that "if the relator [Matranga] has the rights in which he asserts, and, if by the refusal of the District Judge to recognize and enforce them, he is prevented from hearing his defence [*sic*]…the same may be inquired into on an appeal and justice can then be done." The Supreme Court thus refused to overturn the lower court's decision.

Continued legal maneuvering made for good press and stressed the resilience and genius of the defense team. The Committee of the Fifty, the august body mandated by Mayor Shakspeare to investigate not only Chief Hennessy's murder but also the existence of secret Italian societies within the city of New Orleans, found itself at the center of controversy and became the focus of a legal argument that could have freed the defendants. On December 19, 1890, Adams and Semmes filed motions for subpoenas duces tecum "for the minutes, records, oaths, and vouchers of the committee, and for all affidavits referring to the accused," and motions to quash based on a newly discovered partiality. The judge granted some of the defense requests and denied others. In the annals of legal history, this ruling set a precedent whereby non-congressional committees such as the Committee of the Fifty benefited from their clandestine meetings. Another point of legal contention raised by the defense team came with the discovery that "because Walmsley and [Simon] Hernshiem, members of the Grand Jury, were also members of the Committee of the Fifty…[the committee] had subscribed money for their prosecution." Despite the blatant conflict of interest, the court refused to quash the indictments and scheduled the trial of the suspected killers for February 1891.

Jury selection for the trial of the suspected murderers of Chief Hennessy began on February 16, 1891, before respected jurist Judge Joshua Baker, Section A, Criminal District Court. The prosecution and defense interviewed over one thousand potential jurors. Following several challenges, on the twelfth day of the proceedings, the opposing sides compromised on the jury's makeup: J.M. Seligman, a jeweler, jury foreman; John Berry Jr., solicitor for a flour company; Henry L. Trouchet, clerk; Arnold F. Willie, grocery store clerk; Charles Heyob, clerk; Charles Boessen, clerk; Solomon J. Mayer, real estate developer; Walter D. Livaudais, railroad clerk; William G. Leahy, machinist; E.J. Donegan, moulder; William Yochum, grocer; and William McKessey, occupation unknown. None of the jurors were of Italian descent. Six weeks of testimony began, and subsequently, 319 prosecution witnesses testified by the beginning of March 1891. Among the most integral, Deputy Coroner Dr. Paul Archinard, reading from an earlier autopsy report, described Hennessy's wounds in great detail. Reciting from his report, Dr. Archinard stated, "Death was caused by internal hemorrhage as a result of gunshot wounds…one wound situated three inches below the nipple…the bullet fractured right rib traveled from left to right and a little downward perforating the liver…There were three fatal wounds, one through the liver, one through the stomach, and one through the intestines, all very large."

Zachary Foster, an African American near the scene of Hennessy's shooting, "identified Scaffedi, Marchesi [sic], Monasterio, and Politz [sic] as the men who had fired the deadly fusillade into the body of the late chief." Spectators in the gallery reacted with shock to Foster's testimony, hearing for the first time that a witness identified the actual shooters. The state eventually abandoned its case against Sebastiano Incardona, and Judge Baker offered an acquittal for Charles Matranga because of lack of evidence.

At one moment in the proceedings, Adams, Henriques and Semmes cringed when Manuel Polizzi exhibited signs of a psychological breakdown while sitting at their defense table. One observer present in the courtroom noted, "At 11:00 [a.m.] he was violent and made a dash for the window overlooking the street." The defense attorneys hoped that Polizzi's outburst would not dampen their chances of acquittal for their clients. Deputy Sheriffs in the courtroom tried to regain control of Polizzi with some difficulty and eventually removed the defendant back to jail. Later, Polizzi tried to fire his attorney and continue the trial without legal representation. Judge Baker allowed M. Theard, Polizzi's counsel, to resign, but Adams, Semmes and Henriques "advised" their unbalanced client. Polizzi's violent streak continued throughout the day of the trial. The coroner examined him "but could not positively determine whether Polizzi was suffering from nervous prostration or insanity." A woman purported to be Polizzi's wife told newspaper reporters that her husband had returned home at 7:30 p.m. on the night of the murder. On March 4, 1891, this same woman visited Polizzi at the Orleans Parish Prison and told him "she would have nothing more to do with him, as he betrayed his countrymen."

Despite the excitement Polizzi brought to the courtroom, both sides submitted their cases to the jury on March 11, 1891. District Attorney Luzenberg rested the state's case with a brief recap of the evidence and declared in his closing statement, "It is time this thing should stop. That is why we are here. It is time that the city's good name be saved. If the jury has no reasonable doubt it must find the accused guilty." Attorney Thomas J. Semmes provided the closing statement for the defense, eloquently arguing that there was "no divinity hedged around Mr. Hennessy to make his assassination different from anyone else." Semmes elaborated that the prosecution wanted the jury to believe that "Hennessy was killed as a representative of the law" and questioned whether any proof existed that substantiated that assertion. The magnification of Hennessy's assassination in comparison with others in that period should not, according to Semmes, have any influence on the jury's decision whatsoever: "It was only an ordinary assassination and the same rules of evidence and the same method of reaching a verdict [should] be observed concerning it as in any other case."

After the closing arguments of attorneys Semmes and Adams, Judge Baker charged the jury to carefully review the evidence presented. At the same time, Baker ordered an acquittal for Charles Matranga due to lack of evidence.

The jury deliberated for two days without a break and, on March 13, 1891, returned with its verdict. The facial expressions of the accused before the chief clerk read the verdict were noted as "look[s] of infinite woe." The jury voted not guilty for six of the defendants but could not agree on a verdict for the remaining three. Ten minutes after reading the verdict, "the accused were taken downstairs by the back way, put in vans and driven to the parish prison where they were safely landed behind bars." William Grant, U.S. attorney in New Orleans at the time of the trial, wrote a report on the trial to his superiors: "The evidence in the case against them [defendants] submitted to the jury is voluminous, covering 800 pages of typewriting and in detail...Both as a whole is exceedingly unsatisfactory, and is not, in my mind, conclusive one way or the other." Grant subsequently averred that he found no evidence that the defendants belonged to a criminal underworld "or any association of a similar character in the city."

Citizens of New Orleans convinced themselves, along with some help from the local media, that the jury had determined the innocence of the accused prior to hearing the testimony and reviewing the evidence. One unidentified juror "had the charming confrontery to declare that the jury did not believe there was a thing in this city as a Mafia Society, despite the fact that the papers for the last twenty years have been publishing accounts of midnight on our streets." The clamor for "justice" criticized the twelve men and praised the state's evidence as well-deserving of a guilty verdict. The bloody clothes Hennessy wore that night, the mostly unreliable eyewitness identifications and an alleged admission by the jury foreman, Seligman, that he convinced the jury to acquit all demonstrated to a prejudiced public that the Italian prisoners deserved incarceration at the very least, if not the death penalty. Interviewed by a local newspaper, Seligman claimed to have "kept things straight."

Seligman paid dearly for his actions. The local stock exchange and men's gymnastics club expelled him, citing that "by his action as a juror in the Hennessy case [he] evidently contributed to defy justice." Even Seligman's brother dissolved the partnership the two held in a jewelry exchange. With his livelihood gone, Seligman attempted to leave town. Before he could make his escape, "a mob captured him on the way to the station, but he was rescued by the police, and has been concealed by his friends."

Because so many questioned the impartiality of the Hennessy jury, a grand jury was seated to investigate the former's behavior. At the conclusion of this investigation, the grand jury surmised that several parties approached the jurors with regards to bribes for acquittal and maintained that anyone attempting to bribe the jurors would have had no trouble doing so, as Judge Baker failed to sequester the jurors during the trial. Investigators concluded that jury members were visited at their homes or stopped on the way to the courtroom in attempts to sway their verdict through bribery. The body never mentioned who might have been the purveyors of the bribery.

However controversial the Hennessy jury's decision and the rumors of bribery were, the verdict infuriated the people of the city. Throughout the night of March 13, various meetings took place in the city calling for a plan of vengeance against the Italians who allegedly murdered the chief. On the following day, some of the city's most influential citizens and leaders announced in an advertisement

MASS MEETING!

All good citizens are invited to attend a mass meeting on SATURDAY, March 14, at 10 o'clock a. m., at Clay Statue, to take steps to remedy the failure of justice in the HENNESSY CASE. Come are ared for action.

John C. Wickliffe,
B. F. Glover,
J. G. Pepper,
C. E. Rogers,
F. E. Hawes,
Raymond Hayes,
L. E. Cenas,
John M. Parker, Jr.
Harris H. Lewis,
Septime Villere,
Wm. M. Railey,
Lee McMillan,
C. E. Jones,
J. F. Queeny,
D. h. Calder,
Thomas Henry,
James Lea McLean,
Felix Couturie,
T. D. Wharton,
Frank B. Hayne,
J. G. Flower,
James Clarke,
Thomas H. Kelley,
H. B. Ogden,
Ulric Atkinson,
A. Baldwin, Jr.,
A. E. Blackmar,
John V. Moore,
Wm. T. Pierson,
C. L. Steval,
E. T. Leche,

W. S. Parkerson,
Henry Dickson Bruns,
Wm. H. Deeves,
Richard S. Venables,
Samuel B. Merwin,
Omer Villere,
H. L. Favrot,
T. D. Mather,
James T. Mulvey,
Emile Du re,
W. P. Curtiss,
Chas. J. Hanlett,
T. S. Barton,
C. J. Forstall,
J. Moore Wilson,
Hugh W. Brown,
C. Harrison Parker,
Edwar H. Farrar,
J. C. Aby,
Rud. Hahne,
C. A. Walecher,
W. Mosby,
Chas. M. Barnwell,
H. R. Labouisse,
Walter D. Denegre,
George Denegre,
R. H. Hornbeck,
S. P. Walmsley,
E. H. Pierson,
James D. Houston,

The mass meeting announcement following the acquittal of eleven Italians for the murder of New Orleans police chief David C. Hennessy. *Daily Picayune*, March 14, 1890. *Courtesy of the* Times Picayune.

that "all good citizens are invited to attend a meeting on Saturday, March 14, at 10:00 o'clock am, at the Clay Statue to take steps to remedy the failure of justice in the Hennessy case. Come prepared for action."

Early the next morning, the crowd began to gather. Estimates of over ten thousand people congregated at the Clay Statue at the foot of Canal Street.

Prominent businessman W.F. Parkerson, future law enforcement consultant to the city; Walter Denegre; and successful attorney John C. Wickliffe used ethnic vitriol to incite the crowd. Parkerson spoke first, pronouncing, "In the midst of a peaceful community an officer of the law was stricken down by a brand of midnight assassins…the jury has failed [and] now the people has [*sic*] to act." Denegre followed Parkerson. "I charge," Denegre began, "that the jury has been tampered with…I am not after the Italians or Sicilians as a race. I want every man who murdered David Hennessy punished." After Denegre concluded, Wickliffe then stepped forward to address the gathering:

> *If such action as the acquittal of these assassins is to be further tolerated, if nothing is done to forcibly portray the disapproval of the public of this infamous verdict, not one man can expect to carry his life safe in the face of the organized assassination that so powerfully exists in our midst as to openly set law and order at defiance…Fall under the leadership of W.S. Parkerson. James D. Houston will be your First Lieutenant, and I, J.C. Wickliffe, will be your Second Lieutenant.*

The Italian consul in New Orleans, Pascale Corté, saw the advertisement in the newspaper and feared the worst. He hurriedly made his way to Mayor Shakspeare's office, but Corté noted that Mayor Shakspeare was nowhere to be found. Louisiana attorney general George Rogers and Orleans Parish criminal sheriff Gabriel Villeré arrived at the mayor's office. Since he couldn't meet with the mayor, Corté left with Sheriff Villeré and Attorney General Rogers to a house on the outskirts of the city where Governor Nicholls happened to be visiting at the time.

Governor Nicholls sat at the breakfast table as Corté entered with Villeré and Rogers. The consul presented his reservations concerning the advertisement. Governor Nicholls stated that he had seen the advertisement but "was convinced there was no danger of violence" and saw no need to interfere with city affairs. Nicholls suggested that Corté breakfast with him and wait for a call from the Pickwick Club, where Shakspeare often frequented. Nicholls stated he had left a message for Shakspeare to call. Corté sat nervously but did not eat. The consul then looked at his watch and noticed that the appointed hour of the mass meeting had passed.

By the time Corté made it to Nicholls's lodgings, Parkerson, Denegre and Wickliffe had led the crowd through Congo Square (the present-day location of Armstrong Park) on North Rampart Street on their way to the Old Parish Prison at Basin and Treme Streets. Hearing the rumblings,

The Clay Statue, where the meeting of the New Orleans citizens took place prior to heading to the Old Orleans Parish Prison, March 1891. *Courtesy of the New Orleans Public Library, City Archives/Special Collections Division, Irene Wainwright, Archivist.*

Captain Lemuel Davis, commander in charge of the officers at the prison, readied his men.

An eyewitness in the crowd related the following:

> *When the crowd poured down the Orleans, the advance guard, armed with shotguns and improved Winchesters, and numbering three hundred men, at once took possession of the main entrance of the prison and demanded of Capt. Lem Davis permission which he did not disposed [sic] to grant, and then messengers were immediately dispatched for axes and crowbars and picks which were soon at hand and then commenced a furious pounding upon the massive front gate but it did not yield to the blows showered upon it.*

Captain Davis moved the nineteen male prisoners to the female side of the prison. The heavily barricaded gates of the prison on the Orleans Street side remained the focal point of the mob's push into the prison. Another eyewitness at the prison recounted:

> *Some of the brave among the representatives of the Mafia wanted to die fighting for their lives, and they pleaded for weapons with which to defend themselves, and when they could not find these they sought a hiding place…Soon there was*

a crash and the door gave way, and in an instant armed citizens were pouring through the small opening, while a mighty shout went up from 10,000 throats.

When the gates finally collapsed and the crowd rushed in, one of the men who entered ahead of the rest turned to the crowd and asked if any of the men could recognize the suspected assassins. "We do not want to shed innocent blood," he said.

Once inside the gate, the mob marched up the front stairs of the prison. An old woman pointed them to another set of stairs, and they made their way to the women's side of the prison. There they heard footsteps from behind the door leading to the female side and, determined to discover the Italians, broke down the door and found another winding staircase leading to the courtyard of the women's side. There, Jim Caruso, Monasterio, Comitez and Traina cornered themselves, waiting for the retribution of the bloodthirsty crowd. When the suspected assassins tried to escape through an open gate, someone shouted, "Give it to them!" The crowd opened fire without remorse. When the smoke cleared in the courtyard, all six unarmed prisoners lay dead.

Elsewhere in the prison, the mob cornered Scaffedi, the elder Marchese and Joseph Macheca. Scaffedi received a rifle wound above his right eye that tore away the top of his skull. He fell dead instantly. Antonio Marchese tried to run but tripped over Scaffedi's body and fell to the ground. At this time, Marchese received buckshot to his forehead and shoulders. He struggled to regain his footing and ran down a corridor stairway, slamming a door behind him. He struggled to keep the door shut, but too many of his pursuers pulled at the door. The mob entered and fired two shotgun blasts at Marchese. He fell to the ground dead. Joseph Macheca was later discovered with Marchese, his corpse riddled with gunshots, a small wound from one of those shots through his head behind his right ear.

The mob next turned to another area of the prison where they searched for other Italians. Manuel Polizzi tried to make his way through the front of the prison in a crowd of people. Captured by the crowd, he was lynched from a lamppost on St. Ann Street. The crowd next dragged prisoner Bagnetto out of the main entrance as well and hanged him by the neck from a giant oak tree in front of the prison. The crowd used his corpse for target practice, causing a "thud" with every round striking the lifeless body.

By the end of the slaughter, nine of the prisoners lay dead or mortally wounded in the courtyard of the prison. While the other two bodies hung outside, their faces contorted in death, Loretto Comitez's head had been blown off from a shotgun blast. Charles Traina received gunshot wounds that tore open his chest. Big Jim Caruso was first shot in the neck, which slowed him down in his dash for safety, and then a volley cut him to pieces in the prison courtyard. A massive volley of shotgun pellets felled Rocco Garachi; he collapsed to his knees and bled to death. Monasterio writhed from the wound to his throat until an old man from the crowd ended the cobbler's suffering with one shot to the head. Charles Matranga survived the massacre with only a bullet wound to the arm, hiding underneath one of his dead compatriots until the crowd vacated the prison. With the massacre concluded, the crowd hailed Parkerson, Denegre and Wickliffe as heroes and left the devastation in their wake.

After his failed attempts to see Mayor Shakspeare, Corté went to the prison as fast as his carriage could take him and witnessed the aftermath of the carnage. After briefly surveying the crowd's handiwork, Corté immediately climbed back into his carriage and made haste to his consulate, where he sought refuge. Three men waited on the front step of his office building and attempted to rush the diplomat, forcing the consul to unholster his weapon to ward off the men. During the next three days, cries of "Kill the Italian!" rang through the streets of the city. Corté subsequently reported the sad news to Baron Fava in Washington: "Mob led by members of the Committee of the Fifty took possession of the jail; killed eleven prisoners; three Italians, others naturalized. I hold Mayor responsible. Fear further murders. I also am in great danger. Reports follow."

The Italian settlement in New York gathered in various meeting places and planned to lodge protests against the lynchings. Charles Barsotti, editor of *Il Progresso Italo-Americano* newspaper, commented on March 15 "that a mob should break down the gates of the jail and kill these men in any event, but the more because they were fairly tried, and a jury made up of citizens had by their verdict decided that there was not sufficient evidence to convict them." In Chicago, Italian residents demanded more than just resolutions of peaceful protest. They clamored for the Italian government to recognize the outrage "of the Federal government satisfactory reparation [and] the severe punishment of the leaders, who were active in breaking the laws guaranteeing the right of citizenship and hospitality." Italians strongly voiced their concerns to Consul Corté in New Orleans as well.

Reactions to the lynching of the Italians brought outrage from all over the United States. From San Francisco, on March 18, 1891: "At a meeting of Italian citizens here tonight, the speakers denounced the New Orleans lynching as a bloody crime and barbarous butchery." In Boston at Faneuil Hall, three thousand Italian residents vented their anger at the lynching. From Nashville, Italian inhabitants "passed resolutions of sympathy with the Italians in New Orleans," protested to the American and Italian governments

Monument to New Orleans police officers who were killed in the line of duty, located in front of police headquarters at South Broad and White Streets, New Orleans, Louisiana. Hennessy's name appears approximately halfway down on the monument. *Courtesy of the author.*

and demanded some sort of monetary compensation for the families of the murder victims.

Some citizens in New Orleans reacted openly with approval concerning the murders. Members of the Cotton Exchange adopted a resolution endorsing the actions of the mob: "While we deplore at all times the resort to violence, we consider the action taken by the citizens this morning to be proper and justifiable." John P. Richardson, owner of a dry goods store in New Orleans, declared, "It looks bad on its face to those from there, but people who are acquainted with the status of affairs can do nothing but commend the action taken." Richardson continued, "They [Italians] are treacherous, revengeful, and seek their revenge in most foul and cowardly manners."

Mayor Shakspeare received several letters of praise from people all over the nation expressing their approval at his inaction to prevent the lynching. W.R. Coats from Kalamazoo, Michigan, wrote, "I hold that the taking of the lives of those Maffia [*sic*] murderers on the 1ˢᵗ [fourteenth] of March was a righteous act and in the interest of <u>true</u> <u>liberty</u> and <u>American</u> <u>advancement</u>." In another postcard, T. Garland in New York compared the mayor to the "pearl" of English literature when he stated, "We need a Shakspeare here to create a language that the leaders of thirty thousand thieves can understand." Another letter, this one from San Francisco, displayed a fervent patriotism as its writers, J.H. Porterfield and A.C. Rulafson, again compared Shakspeare to the bard when they declared: "As Americans, we beg to present our sincere thanks for the able manner in which you 'stayed at home and attended to your own private business,' while the citizens of your city avenged the insult to our flag; the assassination of Hennessy, and the debauchery of the Courts and Jury. The world has produced two great Shakespeares—the English poet, and the American Mayor."

Chapter 4

The Likely Suspects

(Who Benefited from Hennessy's Death?)

*All his adult life, [Dominick] O'Malley was a foe to liars and those who tried
to outsmart the police, especially if they did it better than he could.*
—*obituary of Dominick O'Malley*

The final report of the grand jury, dated May 6, 1891, stated, "Careful observers testify with special reference to the marked inattention of the jury as the witnesses submitted their evidence—a conduct most unbecoming and fraught with the gravest consequences." The investigators concluded that the jurors ignored evidence presented before them and relied on the media of the day and innuendo to make their final determination. The assembly also held suspicions that the jurors had been "approached" prior to the proceedings; they received nocturnal visits at their homes, were caught in the hallways of the courthouse during recesses or were met on their way to court in order for offers to be made for their "cooperation." The grand jury also accused the defense team of improprieties, suggesting that a "list of five hundred talisman in the Hennessy case was in the office of O'Malley and Adams at 11:00 am, Sunday morning, February 22, 1891," just prior to the beginning of the trial, providing ample opportunity to identify and bribe jury members. The grand jury suspected Dominick O'Malley, the private investigator, of concocting a bribery conspiracy to acquit the eleven Italians.

O'Malley's notoriety during the grand jury investigation into the killings of the eleven Italians in the Old Parish Prison implied libelous and unsubstantiated allegations of shady dealings and less-than-legal actions.

The grand jury surmised that if O'Malley were capable of illegal actions in the past, what would deter him from "fixing" this jury during one of the most important trials in American history? To support their argument, investigators for the grand jury held that O'Malley possessed a complete list of the jurors in the trial due to his connections in the district attorney's office.

The Shakspeare administration had its own means of gaining information concerning the defense strategy. According to the grand jury, Thomas C. Collins, an officer working undercover with Adams, Semmes, Henriques and O'Malley, engaged in spying for Mayor Shakspeare on the defense team and submitted reports that revealed defense strategies during the trial. Based on Collins's accounts, he reported to the grand jury:

> *In the attempts to influence the talisman of the Hennessy case no visible act was committed, and we fully realize the difference between a crime committed by words only and what are known as visible acts, which might be witnessed by other persons and tell the tale of a crime. In the attempts to influence talismen, and the successful part of it, whispered words conveyed the insinuation or directly offered the money influence.*

With this passage, the grand jury admitted the evidence it relied on to be hearsay, and closer examination of this report as a reliable historical document serves only to question the validity and investigative methods of this body.

With O'Malley accused of jury tampering and attempted bribery despite a lack of substantial exculpatory evidence, the grand jury went beyond the scope of its investigative powers and steadfastly maintained that a conspiracy to derail the wheels of justice had occurred with the acquittal of the eleven Italians. Although O'Malley's past did render it feasible that he may have played a part in the jury tampering, the word of an informant, Thomas Collins, stood between O'Malley and a lengthy jail sentence. Examination of O'Malley's reputation in detail deserves attention in order to understand the reasoning of the grand jury investigators.

In addition to the past charges, the grand jury investigating the Hennessy trial and the lynchings also relied on Dominick O'Malley's history of settling disputes with weapons instead of diplomacy. The sense of a lack of protection of the law prompted denizens to defend themselves, and O'Malley, who certainly made a few enemies in his time, was no different. His facing of mortal situations became legendary. O'Malley once made derogatory remarks concerning a police reporter from a city newspaper. When O'Malley went to the reporter's residence to confront the man, he "was about to enter the man's front door; he saw the man standing across the street, pistol in hand. O'Malley searched for his own—and remembered he left his on the dresser that morning." He approached the armed man and, in front of an eyewitness, snatched the gun from the man's hands. A later incident saw O'Malley and another newspaperman exchanging gunshots with each other on a busy New Orleans street. Each emptied their revolvers and received serious wounds. Both ended up in local hospitals, but only O'Malley walked out alive.

Over the course of his life, O'Malley exhibited no reluctance in the use of fist or firearm. The only time O'Malley demonstrated any fear came at the end of the Hennessy trial with the acquittal of the eleven Italians. Besides demanding the blood of the Italians, William Parkerson's speech at the Clay Statue on March 14 also called for O'Malley's demise. O'Malley actually stood in the crowd that day, heard Parkerson's charges and hurried away before anyone recognized him. A local billiard hall owner saw O'Malley hurrying through the streets and offered him protection under his roof. O'Malley unquestioningly accepted.

The grand jury's supposition that O'Malley played an integral part in a conspiracy to acquit the eleven Italians seemed contrived based on his reputation. His involvement with the trial raised suspicions, and because of his tattered past, O'Malley became the scapegoat for an embarrassing event in judicial history.

The grand jury noted, "From our own experience and knowledge…a large part of the Italian colony in this city is recognized as a worthy class. They do not indulge freely in the use of beer or alcoholic drinks. Fairly industrious, those in the city soon save up a few dollars, more by the strictest frugality than otherwise, and soon are doing something on their own account." Even though it made use of the word "Mafia" repeatedly throughout the report, the underlying subtext of the report displayed bias toward Italians as a whole.

As mentioned previously, the city seated the Committee of the Fifty to investigate the existence of secret societies operating within New Orleans. The committee based its conclusions on the above and presented a finished response to a report allegedly given to them by Consul Pascale Corté. This report supposedly contained the registration papers of Antonio Bagnetto, one of the eleven Italian victims of the lynching on March 14, which included "the imprint of a seal which he [Corté] informed us, was the seal of the Mafia." At this point in time, one would have to ask, why would a member of the Mafia, suspiciously known for its secret manipulations and violence in American history, announce his affiliation with this secret society? This report, along with the grand jury's rendition of events, lacks historical credibility to determine the true identity of the killer, or killers, responsible for the murder of the chief. The report is sufficient, however, to show the forces of something more sinister beneath all the declarations of legitimacy.

Considering the findings of the Committee of the Fifty, Dominick O'Malley may have possessed the opportunity and access to the jury, but what would be his motive for seeing Hennessy dead and the Italians set free?

James D. Houston, successful New Orleans political sui generis and businessman, was heralded as being a man of "unflinching courage and heroic fortitude." Born in St. Louis, Missouri, Houston's father moved the family to New Orleans when the young Houston was only eight years old. "Donny," as his childhood friends called him, impressed his friends with his "remarkable sagacity and dauntless courage." Houston wanted to pursue a career in the maritime industry, but a broken leg dampened his hopes of engaging in that endeavor. During the Civil War, Houston worked in the quartermaster corps, and after the war, in 1869, New Orleans criminal sheriff Jules A. Massicot appointed Houston as chief deputy.

In his capacity as chief deputy, Houston killed his first man on a hot day in August 1871. While performing court duty one day, the judge ordered that an irate spectator, Arthur Guerin, be escorted out of the court building. Once outside the building, accounts detail that Guerin drew his weapon and fired wildly. Houston drew his weapon and returned fire, mortally wounding Guerin. Guerin succumbed to his wounds the next day. Police charged Houston with the murder. After a short trial, the jury acquitted him. Houston's notoriety increased after the Guerin murder trial.

In the 1870s, the people of Orleans Parish elected Houston sheriff. He occupied that position for a short time and then resigned to become state tax collector for the First District of New Orleans. Houston exhibited the demeanor of "conservative attire and Victorian manner [which] reflected antebellum southern aristocracy," yet he never hesitated to demonstrate the brutal strength and control that could be found only through the barrel of a gun. In one particular incident, Houston became embroiled in the death of a respected police officer and further solidified his reputation as a man of intense principle.

Elections in the New Orleans area, and Louisiana for that matter, between the end of the Civil War and the 1920s were incidents in which violence required only a minimum of provocation. Rival political factions often hired "toughs" to patrol precinct polls and terrorize voters to cast ballots for one candidate or the other. On December 14, 1883, a fight erupted in the Seventh Ward as citizens cast their votes for the gubernatorial race. Houston, as tax collector, hovered at the precinct because of his affiliation with one of the candidates, Samuel D. McEnery. Houston accepted the responsibility for becoming McEnery's chairman of the Executive Campaign Committee and sought to observe the returns at the lowest level. Police officers patrolled the polling center to ensure no trouble occurred. An eyewitness at the precinct that day recalled a scuffle between the police and several people attempting to vote. During the confusion, a Mr. Seyrouth "saw Houston draw his revolver and fire, although he does not know to whom the bullet was aimed." After the smoke cleared, three men lay dead, including police captain Michel J. Fortier; Gus Reneaud, superintendent of streets in the Seventh Ward; and Eugene Masson, a deputy constable. Three other men suffered non-lethal wounds, and onlookers transported them to the hospital. Houston became a wanted man as police issued warnings to all precincts to detain him on sight.

Captain Fortier's death, though made to appear as a fracas gotten out of hand, occurred because of his opinionated personality. One opinion stated:

> He [Fortier] was a clear-headed and outspoken man. Throughout the canvass he had expressed himself with vigor and with point. He came before the people in the columns of the press and on the stump...It was impossible either to bribe or intimidate him. Death only could lower his strong arm and silence his eloquent voice. He was the unsparing enemy of bad men, and they hated him as only bad men can hate.

The media praised Captain Fortier as the "Champion of Popular Liberty." As the press continued to memorialize the fallen policeman, Houston turned himself in to authorities when he learned there were warrants sworn out for his arrest.

Houston issued a statement to the press claiming he had shot Captain Fortier in self-defense. He asserted that his presence at the polls on that day reflected his duties as the chairman of the Executive Campaign Committee. He was in the Seventh Ward to receive any complaints about the voting process or to deal with any other problems that might arise. In his confession, Houston stated:

> *During my stay near the poll, a disturbance occurred, followed by pistol shots. Moving from the spot where the disturbance was going on, and while walking across Morales Street, I suddenly found myself confronted by Capt. Fortier, and within a short distance of him. He held a pistol in his hand, and instantly, without provocation or warning, fired point blank at me, the ball striking my breast fully and squarely, and leaving me under the impression that it entered my body.*

Houston maintained that he returned fire and left the scene rather hurriedly. To dispel any suggestions that Captain Fortier died as the result of a conspiracy to silence him, Houston stated that he "deplored" the incident, but "it is consolation to me to reflect that the affair was unsought, unexpected, and totally undesired on my part." Houston counted on the statements of "reputable" political allies to substantiate his actions during the fray. However, one thing could not be dismissed: police determined Captain Fortier's weapon had only "one barrel discharged." With his claim of self-defense, the judge later released Houston to attend the Democratic State Convention in Baton Rouge. Despite his "confession," Houston proved his powerful political connections. He missed the convention, but a judge later dropped the charges.

The next year, a New York political boss, John Kelly, invited Houston to speak at the Democratic State Convention in Cleveland, Ohio. Houston became heavily involved with the Young Men's Democratic Association in New Orleans. Houston's activities after 1880 reflect someone who was "averse to any notoriety of any kind, and, notwithstanding his identification with the party faction, he always preferred to take up his position behind the scenes." Houston stayed behind the scenes, lending his name only to organizations that advocated violence, without any suspicion of his complicity in the planning or execution of any plan that dominated the thinking of business concerns—until 1890.

Houston fought for economic supremacy among his colleagues and fellow capital investors. He perceived a threat to his financial well-being as a result of the Italians staking a claim on the New Orleans docks and capitalizing on their labor and expertise in trading commodities. Therefore, he took serious notice of the Italians and devised a plan to eliminate roadblocks to his own prosperity. Houston capitalized on the controversial nature of Hennessy's relationship with some of the most influential members of the Italian community (whether Mafioso or not) to engineer a takeover of the businesses needed to sustain his empire.

Houston and O'Malley had survived many onslaughts and reacted in the most impulsive manner rather than seeking diplomatic solutions. They therefore appear to be the two most likely suspects, working in concert yet unaware of each other's designs, who could have not only planned the death of Hennessy and the Italians but also controlled the outcomes, relying on the anti-Italian sentiments of the city. O'Malley sought retribution as a matter of revenge. In his function as a private investigator with the defense team, O'Malley could have controlled the outcome that best served both him and Houston. At the point of his acquittal, O'Malley's role ended. Hennessy was dead, and a jury pronounced the eleven Italians not guilty. Houston had to see his designs to their conclusion.

As previously mentioned, U.S. attorney William Grant stated that the evidence against the eleven Italians fell short of any conclusive proof. Houston had to do something or his greatest competitor, Macheca, could walk away a free man and continue to provide more competition for Houston's interests. Houston relied on the anti-Italian and Mafia fear to organize the "Mass Meeting" on March 14, 1891. Houston led the group (from behind the scenes, of course) on that fateful day to the Old Orleans Parish Prison, seeking to play his part as benefactor of the white race in New Orleans and to solidify his business interests. Macheca, in particular, received notable attention, and the mob made sure he did not escape their wrath. Houston needed Macheca eliminated in order to perfect his arrangement and in order to ensure the success of the murders. Houston associated any justification of the lynching with the survival of democracy and the anti-Italian bias that was prevalent at the time of the lynchings.

Later in his life, O'Malley sought to diminish the negativity surrounding his name. Eventually, he purchased the *New Orleans Item*, turning the failing newspaper around and increasing circulation. He later sold the newspaper at a sizeable profit. But O'Malley's influence ended with serious libel charges when he denigrated Mayor Martin Behrman in 1904. Seeking to end the controversy in his life, O'Malley sold the *Item* in 1907. Later that year, a physician diagnosed him with Bright's disease, an affliction of the liver caused from years of drinking alcohol. After selling the *Item* and the doctor's diagnosis, O'Malley went to work briefly with the Fish and Game Department and then purchased the short-lived newspaper the *New Orleans American.* "O'Malley's [illness] compelled him to give up his activities and go to Touro Infirmary. He underwent an operation at that institution but little hope at any time was held out for his recovery, due to his weakened condition." O'Malley passed away on November 27, 1920.

Although Houston occupied several other politically connected positions, his crowning achievement in business was the Louisiana Construction and Improvement Company, an endeavor he controlled until his death in 1894. This company signified the crowning achievement in his business domination over the Italians, in particular Joseph P. Macheca. Macheca ran businesses through the docks, and Houston needed those business interests to establish a monopoly on both the profits made and the labor used. The Louisiana Construction and Improvement Company, which came into existence immediately after the lynching in 1891, procured leases from those who desired to utilize the New Orleans wharves for import and export purposes. With this company, Houston maintained a monopoly on those leases.

Hollywood dramatized a meeting between Houston and Macheca in the movie *Vendetta* (1999), produced by HBO and based (loosely) on supposed true events. Macheca, expertly played by Joachim de Alameida, and Houston, played by veteran actor Christopher Walken, meet in Macheca's office, and Houston makes Macheca an offer (that the latter refuses) to sell his businesses at much lower prices than they are worth. Perhaps the meeting did occur, but the details probably are lost to history. This would explain the expeditious manner with which Macheca's interests absorbed into Houston's businesses after his death.

Chapter 5

Italy Threatens War

The killing yesterday of defenseless Italian prisoners, a part of whom was acquitted and a part not yet tried, has affected the civilized world.
—*Pascale Corté, Italian consul in New Orleans, March 15, 1891*

While Mayor Joseph Shakspeare received praises for his indifference toward the massacre, envoys of the U.S. State Department attempted to explain away the behavior of Louisiana officials to representatives of the Italian government who saw the massacre as a major slight against their compatriots. The actions of both countries evoked feelings of nationalism while raising questions of international law concerning foreign nationals residing in other countries. The diplomatic exchanges continued as Italy reacted to the nonchalance of Louisiana and American officials over the murder of eleven Italians.

Even before the trial and the lynching, American officials questioned the validity of Italy's claim that the indicted Italians were actually citizens of that country, or "whether or not the persons now under indictment for that offense are naturalized citizens of the United States." At least one American official, Assistant Secretary of State William F. Wharton, made the request for information concerning the citizenship of the indicted men. United States attorney in New Orleans William Grant investigated Wharton's request and reported that although born in Italy, Antonio Marchese, Manuel Polizzi, Carlos Traina, Loretto Comitez, Pietro Monasterio, Sebastiano Incardona, Salvatore Sunzeri and Rocco Garachi did "not appear from any record to have been naturalized." Based on Grant's report, the Italian government held cause to show concern over the incarceration of the prisoners on such a serious charge. Italy declared that the prisoners deserved fair treatment based on treaties signed by both countries.

A report from George W. Flynn, supervisor of registration for the Parish of Orleans, stood as the basis for Grant's report. Flynn noted that some of the suspects claimed Italy as their place of birth (some in Sicily) and registered to vote in their respective wards. Registration to vote was contingent on making an open declaration to become a citizen in court. Flynn did not discern whether all the suspects had expressed that desire. Charles Matranga became a citizen of the United States "by virtue of his father's naturalization," and Joseph Macheca claimed Louisiana as his birthplace. The Italian government's legal claims may have been suspect, but its motivation bore merit. Governor Nicholls later claimed to Secretary of State James Blaine that Comitez, Peter Monasterio and Charles Traina were the only Italian subjects murdered by the mob on March 14, 1891.

The Marquis di Rudini, Italian ambassador of state, wrote to Baron Saverio Fava, Italian ambassador to the United States, to "beg to denounce immediately to the U.S. government the atrocious deed in New Orleans." Rudini implored Baron Fava to take steps to protect the Italian colony in New Orleans and strongly advocate the capture and prosecution of those responsible for the lynching. Baron Fava contacted Secretary of State Blaine and lodged a formal protest with Washington. Fava stated that he was compelled "to protest in the most solemn manner against the unjustifiable conduct of the local authorities who not only did not prevent a meeting which was publicly announced the day before, and which left no doubt as to its hostility to the Italians." Baron Fava all but demanded that the federal government exert pressure on Louisiana authorities to investigate the incident thoroughly and bring those responsible to justice. Fava also declared the right of the Italian government to demand reparations for the Italian families of the men killed at the prison. Blaine received Fava's concerns and wrote to Governor Nicholls in Louisiana. Blaine informed the governor of the treaty with Italy that stood under the U.S. Constitution as the "supreme law of the land" that "guarantees to the Italian subjects domiciled in the United States" the same protection from harm of person or property as any citizen of the United States. Blaine also strongly suggested that those responsible for the lynching of the Italians be arrested and brought before the proper authorities where justice could be dispensed through legal means.

On March 26, 1891, Baron Fava wrote to Secretary of State Blaine that the Marquis di Rudini "insisted on the necessity that the Federal government should formally assure him that the murderers of the Italian subjects in New Orleans be brought to justice without further delay, and that an indemnity be granted to the families of the victims." The monthly publication *American Advocate of Peace and Arbitration* opined, "If Louisiana is recalcitrant and fails to punish her criminals and does not ask for help of the general government it is difficult to see how [by] our Constitution the outraged and the weak are to be defended—even though they are citizens of a nation whose subjects are bound by treaty to protect."

Because of the American government's lack of response to the Italian demands, Baron Fava eventually left Washington under orders from Rudini. Fava's hasty departure made Blaine suspect the Italians may have misinterpreted the facts surrounding the incident and the U.S. government's delay in responding. Blaine stated that the demands of the Italian government would be recognized; however, "the United States would not be unduly hurried; nor will it make an answer to any demand until every fact essential to a correct judgment shall have been fully ascertained through legal authority." The Italian parliament was set to reassemble on April 14 and wanted the assurances of the United States government that an agreement could be reached on Italy's demands before the parliament convened.

Governor Nicholls responded to Blaine that "their [the victims'] race or nationality was not a factor in the disturbance." The lack of objectivity and ready provocation to convict (and even kill) the Italians demonstrated the absurdity of Governor Nicholls's remarks. Nicholls's statement certainly would not have calmed the fears of Consul Corté, who witnessed the mob's handiwork firsthand and related his fears to Baron Fava.

The diplomatic channels remained open, but the Italians attempted more coercive means to get the United States to act. Marquis Guglielmo Imperiali di Francavilla, head of the Italian Legation in Washington, D.C., responded to Secretary of State Blaine's steadfast embrace of political protocol. As a representative of the King of Italy, Umberto I, the marquis relayed to Blaine the frustration of the Italian government: "The government of the King of Italy has asked nothing beyond the institution of judicial proceedings through the regular channels. It would have been absurd to claim the punishment of the guilty parties without the warrant of regular judgment. The Italian government now repeats the same demand." Imperiali also reiterated the other Italian demand of reparations to the families of the murdered Italian subjects.

The Italian demands, according to Imperiali, held legal foundations with a treaty concluded between the United States and Italy ratified on November

18, 1871. Entitled the Treaty of Commerce and Navigation, this agreement held that Italian immigrants would enjoy "the most constant protection and security for their persons and property, and shall enjoy in this respect the same rights and privileges as are or shall be granted to the natives…The citizens of either party shall have free access to the courts of justice, in order to maintain and defend their own rights." After a heated exchange between Blaine and Rudini concerning Italy's possible course of action, Blaine wrote to the minister that the Italian interpretation of the treaty and the rights it contains must not be taken literally. Blaine maintained that no matter how civilized a country may appear, it is unable "to secure its own citizens against violence promoted by individual malice or by sudden popular tumult." Blaine's opinion held that those foreigners in the United States would not be considered a "favored class" and therefore must be content with the rights given in the U.S.-Italian agreement. Furthermore, Secretary Blaine conditioned any indemnity to the families of the murdered Italians:

> *If, therefore, it should appear that among those killed by the mob at New Orleans there were some Italian subjects who were resident, or domiciled in the city…and not in violation of our immigration laws…and that the public officers charged with the duty of protecting life and property in that city connived at the work of the mob, or upon proper notice or information of the threatened danger, failed to take any steps for the preservation of the public peace and afterwards to bring the guilty to trial, the President would, under such circumstances, feel that case was established that should be submitted to the consideration of Congress with a view to relief of the families of the Italian subjects who had lost their lives by lawless violence.*

Blaine's assessment of the conditional award of an indemnity to the Italian families who lost loved ones in the massacre did not deter the Italian government from pursuing the matter any further. Italy believed the death of a handful of citizens warranted either reparations for the families or war with the United States. Italy was well on its way to becoming a legitimate world power and postured in such a way as to reflect that belief.

With the rattling of sabers between the United States and Italy, two distinguished members of the U.S. Senate antagonized the situation further. John Sherman, from Ohio, pointed out that Italian officials did not understand the complicated process through which these incidents were negotiated. Senator Sherman believed that Baron Fava displayed impatience throughout the whole negotiating process and Italy made a tremendous mistake in insisting that the United States meet its demands. Senator Watson C. Squire commented that Italy's persistence in settling the matter in its favor could be a punitive act because the United States passed laws against the *padrone* system. Italy's actions, according to Squire, signified the first sign of diplomatic difficulty between the two nations. Squire suggested a rather veiled and clandestine threat that, should Italy choose to make war against the United States, citizens in America would be held hostage and other "retaliatory measures" taken.

Despite the antagonisms of some U.S. lawmakers, rumors persisted about Italian naval mobilization. An Italian officer sent a cablegram he received to an Italian newspaper alerting the naval command at La Spezia, Italy, its largest naval base, to be on alert due to "the recent turn of affairs in America." Additionally, newspapers received reports that a meeting occurred between the Italian minister of marine and chiefs of the general staff in the Italian admiralty. Although no information surfaced as to the substance of the meeting, American authorities surmised Italy was preparing for war.

The newspapers printed whatever information they found stating that the United States diplomatic corps endeavored to satisfy the Italian demands without losing much self-respect. Secretary of State Blaine wrote a letter to the Italian government that Baron Fava's recall and departure had been premature. Blaine stated, "The baron's service here for the last ten years has been distinguished at all times by the most agreeable relations with the Executive Department of this government. The regret of his leaving is enhanced when, as the President believes, he has been recalled under a misapprehension of facts by the Government of Italy." Blaine impressed upon Marquis Imperiali that a complete investigation had yet to reach any conclusions and even if the federal government held jurisdiction over the entire investigation, it could not ensure that the guilty parties would be prosecuted. Blaine knew he was working against the clock because the Italian parliament would reassemble on April 14. It became apparent that the Italian government had tired of the diplomatic excuses.

While the diplomatic jousting continued between the two nations, rumors of war permeated, provoking a reassessment of the nation's military might. More than a year prior to the Hennessy Affair, U.S. secretary of the navy Benjamin F. Tracy issued his annual report for 1890, in which he described the cache of ships built and armaments, strength and strategies that the navy would employ in a military situation. With an arsenal to include "20 battleships, 20 coast and harbor defense vessels, and 60 cruisers," Secretary Tracy prided himself in modernizing the U.S. Navy and showing other nations of the world that the United States was preparing to emerge as a world power.

The Italians had hinted at their military preparedness more than a year before when they reported the results of their newest war craft sea trials: "Information is received that the new Italian torpedo cruiser *Montebello* made a mean of $20\frac{1}{2}$ knots an hour over a fifty-mile course." This new vessel dispersed 741 tons and carried armaments of rapid-fire guns and torpedoes. The Italian minister of marine commented that because of the rapid development of Italy's navy, several of its aged ironclads would be scrapped. Italy also constructed heavy boats—ten large warships and fifteen war frigates—and made that no state secret.

Other world powers questioned the need for such large combat vessels. One observer at the time noted, "It is a question whether Italy has not overdone the matter in her attempts to surpass other powers in the size of her vessels." When compared to the largest class of the British warship at the time, the Inflexible Class, Sir Edward J. Reed of the British Admiralty Naval Construction Board stated that certain characteristics existed between the new Italian vessels as far as size and ordnance. Reed considered the Italian vessels "even more objectionable from want of armored stability than the Ajax and Agememnon type of the British navy."

The wave of ultra-nationalism that swept through the United States and Italy during the course of this international incident gathered steam as newspapers again, in English and Italian, fomented "trouble and inter-ethnic tensions." Cooler heads eventually prevailed, and the Italian government in Rome realized that a military confrontation with the United States would spell a logistical and economic nightmare. Equally concerned, the United States realized it stood alone when it came to a potential confrontation with the Italians. Furthermore, with the volatile nature of European politics in the late nineteenth century, Rome served its purposes better with its navy close to home, and Italy was concerned about potential French aggression. Despite assertions to the contrary, had a war ignited between the United States and Italy, no doubt the conflict would have been costly and protracted.

The Hennessy Affair, the lynching and war cries remained at the forefront of the news and conversations all over the nation. On December 9, 1891, President Benjamin Harrison delivered his third annual address to a joint session of Congress. The New Orleans lynching became a prime focus of the speech:

The lynching at New Orleans in March last of eleven men of Italian nativity by a mob of citizens was a most deplorable and discreditable incident. It did not, however, have its origins in any general animosity to the Italian people, or in disrespect to the government of Italy, with which our relations were of the friendliest character. The fury of the mob was directed against these men as the supposed participants or accessories in the murder of a city officer. I do not allude to this as mitigating in any degree this offense against law and humanity, but only as affecting the international questions which grew out of it.

President Harrison continued his address by urging the enactment of laws whereby federal jurists would recognize the rights of foreigners living in the United States, thus giving federal authorities jurisdiction involving crimes committed either by or against foreigners.

In April 1892, a full year after the murder of the eleven Italians, Secretary of State Blaine wrote to the Marquis Imperiali stating, "The President, feeling that for such an injury there should be ample indemnity, instructs me to tender you 125,000 francs," the total amount to be distributed among the victims' families. Imperiali replied, "Your excellency also expresses the hope that the decision reached by the President will put an end to the unfortunate incident to which that deplorable occurrence gave rise, and that the relations between the two countries will be formerly reestablished." The payment of $24,330.90, in the words of President Harrison, "was accepted by the King of Italy with every manifestation of gracious appreciation, and the incident has been high promotive of mutual respect and good will." Whether the payment was "promotive of respect and good will" to quell the protective voices of a foreign population living in the United States or as a deterrent to war, for the time being, the incident seemed forgotten.

On a national level, the nativist and nationalist protests united the nation into one camp, a meeting of minds that unexpectedly provided cohesion after the destruction of the Civil War. North and South perceived a foreign conflict on an issue dear to both regions, and that threatened to tear apart the very fabric of law and order in America. In an effort to preserve that fabric, normal citizens took the law into their own hands.

White supremacists who once valued the Italian work ethic now sought to degrade the Italian population of Louisiana, especially when it came to their politics. Wrapping themselves in a red, white and blue cloak, the established white political machines of the state viewed the Italian community more as a hindrance to reestablishing white dominance of Louisiana. This ignited subsequent incidents of violence against Italians.

Whoever was responsible for the death of New Orleans police chief David C. Hennessy could never have foreseen the international implications of their actions. With the lynching of the eleven Italians, the case was considered closed and the perpetrators given their just due. Historians and researchers over time have accepted the explanation that the Italians were responsible for the death of the chief and escaped justice, without examining other motives and who might have benefited from the murder.

Chapter 6

Italians Caught in the Middle

With the difficulties between the United States and Italy settled for the time being, the political mechanisms in Louisiana continued as usual, but near the end of the nineteenth century, Italians played a significant part in the political process of the state. The seat of conservative Democratic politics in Louisiana rested in New Orleans with a political machine known as the "Ring." Although this machine stood as the main policymaker for the New Orleans area, a rural movement led by the Bourbons (named for their ideological resemblance to the post–French Revolution Bourbons who advocated a return to ultra-conservative governance of France) shared political ideals with the Ring and worked behind the scenes in the rural parishes, where they focused on two main issues: the aggressive advocacy of white supremacy and conservative fiscal maneuverings. The Bourbons strongly believed, despite their freedom, that blacks were still inferior to whites and it was destined that the smarter race would be in control. With reference to monetary policy, the Democrats had to concern themselves with protection of their life and property. This firmly made apparent that anyone who did not own a great deal of property was not worthy of as much protection as someone who was land-rich. This attitude alienated most whites from the Bourbon platform.

The Bourbon mentality became popular in the cotton-producing parishes of the state, places where whites held the minority. There, the Bourbons identified themselves with rich landholders and portrayed themselves as the guardians of southern racial conventions, while also depicting themselves as men who desired a return to the norm of racial separation that had dominated society in antebellum Louisiana. More importantly, they exhibited a fear of African Americans impressed within the ranks of poor whites. This meant that the Bourbon Democrats felt that the new Italian immigrants should not be included in the political process; African Americans were to be excluded as well. The Italians drew further disdain from white supremacists as they often joined groups that opposed anti-black sentiment.

Blacks, poor whites and Italians in farming communities all over the state faced dire economic straits during the late nineteenth century. Between 1870 and 1897, prices declined sharply for produce the farmers brought to market as a result of widespread overproduction. In addition, revolutions in transportation precipitated an increase in costs for transporting goods to market. Domestic crops faced steep competition from overseas markets, and the prices of these goods dropped correspondingly. Railroad companies monopolized the process of getting crops to market and maximized their profits on the backs of the small-time farmers. The end result of all this was the nation's most dire economic struggle up until that time, with unemployment running high among both blacks and whites. Poor farmers faced widespread debt, and the situation spiraled uncontrollably as long as the "crop-lien system" remained intact. The less the farmer received for his produce, the more the debt grew.

Out of dissatisfaction with this economic system, the Farmers' Alliance arose in Texas in 1876 and quickly spread to Louisiana in order to fight for the poor farmer who loathed corporations and upper-class whites who made decisions based on their own interests. The alliance took it upon itself to educate and organize farmers, advocate agricultural innovations and present a more inviting picture of an agrarian life to those who were not familiar with the desperate and oftentimes difficult struggle for the southern farmer to keep himself and his family from starvation. Although the alliance was not a definitive political party, it made its agenda known throughout Louisiana, especially in the more agrarian regions of the state. It stood for a labor enactment that would improve the system and advocated that public lands be made affordable to small farmers. The alliance also advocated the demise of the convict-lease system.

With the Bourbons bracing themselves for an intense political battle against the rising Republican forces in the state, a political party emerged addressing the concerns of the Farmers' Alliance in Louisiana. The Populist Party arose in response to rising costs of bringing goods to market, the lack of educational opportunities for blacks and poor whites and the corruption and graft associated with Louisiana elections as a direct result of the Democratic Party's struggle to regain white domination. The philosophy of this new movement held "that the government must restrain the selfish tendencies of those who profited at the expense of the poor and needy… [and] that the people, not the plutocrats, must control the government." Populists also embraced efforts to help blacks through their political platform by seeking to end lynching through legislation, end the convict-lease system and fight for African Americans' political rights. The Populists' intentions appeared honorable to blacks seeking equal political status with whites, but in working to politically equalize blacks in the South, old wounds reopened, causing more aggressiveness on the part of white supremacists throughout the South. The Populist ideals that a "willing American worker, be he farmer or laborer, might expect in this land of opportunity not only the chance of work but also, as the rightful reward of his labor, a fair degree of prosperity" attracted a great following in the South, and the party promised to be a formidable adversary to the Democrats in Louisiana.

As far as the Italians were concerned, they believed their economic possibilities fell into line more with the Populists' philosophy than that of the Democrats. The Republicans and Populists fused in 1896 in Louisiana, and as a result, the Democrats wanted to disenfranchise blacks, as they saw the latter as a threat to the return of white domination in the state. But despite their proclamations and actions on behalf of African Americans in the South, the Populists failed to include them to a great extent within their movement, thus alienating them in much the same way as the Democrats.

The Democratic Party of the 1890s in Louisiana, composed mostly of ex-Confederates, formulated a platform for former slave owners to be compensated and to repudiate the constitution of 1868, which they argued created an atmosphere of fraud and corruption and did not express the desires of the people of Louisiana. The constitution of 1868 gave African Americans some gains in racial equality, including, but not limited to, the right to vote and hold office. Regardless of their new political standing, African Americans experienced widespread illiteracy, as whites felt that enrolling them in local schools would ruin the educational system.

African Americans celebrated the constitution of 1868 as their former masters felt the sting of political emasculation at the hands of their former slaves. With the document formulated by the Radical Republicans (whose alleged corrupt policies angered southern whites), any opportunity to reverse or eliminate those policies became tantamount to any Democratic or white supremacist political strategy.

Earlier versions of the Louisiana state constitution addressed the issue of suffrage, but with some ambiguity. In the constitution of 1864, conventioneers did not necessarily seek to disenfranchise blacks. After all, the southern part of the state had been under Union occupation for the better part of the Civil War, and any compromises would benefit blacks due to the nature of negotiating a new constitution. Because of the Union domination of the southern part of the state, New Orleans delegates to the constitutional convention of 1864 ran roughshod over the convention.

General Nathaniel P. Banks, military governor of Louisiana and organizer of the 1864 constitutional convention, hoped that the delegates would grant African Americans the right to vote. The suffrage article in the 1864 constitution provided the right to vote for "every white male who attained the age of twenty-one years, and who has been a resident of the state twelve months preceding the election." Although the constitution did not specifically provide for black suffrage in Louisiana, it did stipulate that "the Legislature shall have the power to pass laws extending to suffrage to such other persons, citizens of the United States, as by military service by taxation to support the government or by intellectual fitness, may be denied entitled thereto." Because of this ambiguity concerning the extension of suffrage to African Americans, none of Louisiana's senators or representatives was seated in Washington, D.C.

Although Italians were not mentioned specifically regarding the suffrage issue in 1864, one delegate did mention the need for foreign peoples on Louisiana soil to speak the language. Nativist feelings reappeared. In a speech to the other conventioneers, John Henderson Jr. questioned why allowances were made for the earlier state constitutions to be translated into French even after Louisiana became an American state in 1812. The question then became whether the new constitution should also be published in the French language. T.B. Thorpe argued that the French people of Louisiana "have ever been loyal, not entered this rebellion, but lived quietly under the United States government." Henderson declared, "I am not prejudiced against this people [French] any more than against the Italians, Portuguese or Spanish, but at the same time, I feel we are an American people, and whatever race they may be, they should, on American soil, learn to speak our language." Part of Henderson's argument stemmed from spending taxpayer money to pay for translators. In the end, nativists lost the argument.

The Louisiana constitution of 1864 faded three years later as the national Congress passed a series of laws entitled the Military Reconstruction Acts. These acts, succinctly, divided the former Confederacy into five military districts, with Louisiana and Texas situated within the Fifth Military District with major general and Civil War hero Philip Sheridan in command. Under these acts, former Rebel states could be readmitted to the Union provided that they "formed a constitution of government in conformity with the Constitution of the United States in all respects." Additionally, each resident over the age of twenty-one was compelled to swear an oath of allegiance to the United States, and adult males that same age would be given the right to vote, regardless of skin color.

The Louisiana constitution of 1868 provided for the equality of all residents and mirrored the United States Constitution in granting citizenship to all residents in the state. It reminded them that "the citizens of this state owe allegiance to the United States; and this allegiance is paramount to that which they owe to the state." Unlike the ambiguity of suffrage in the 1864 constitution, under Reconstruction pressure, the 1868 Louisiana constitution upheld the principles of the Radical Republicans in Congress and, in the process, strengthened the white supremacists' resolve to reverse any political gains blacks may have achieved since emancipation.

With the 1879 constitution, voting rights for blacks essentially stayed the same, but it provided for a public school system where whites and blacks attended separate schools. The new institutions suffered badly from severe underfunding. Moreover, black teachers received much less pay than their white counterparts. Although their voting rights seemed intact for the time being, blacks would have to endure the fallacy of separate but equal.

White supremacy came to the forefront when the disenfranchisement of blacks became the focus of the Louisiana state constitutional convention of 1898. The Democrats of Louisiana believed that blacks could not consider themselves equal to whites in the state. To accomplish the goal of disfranchisement, Governor Murphy J. Foster, elected in 1892, took the view that blacks and poor whites were too ignorant to vote. Governor Foster proposed that suffrage legislation be added to the constitution based on property and educational requirements, meaning that blacks would have to own property or be literate enough to sign their own names in order to vote. The Louisiana House and Senate agreed to the amendment in 1894 and put it on the ballot for the election of 1896. The amendment served a twofold purpose: first, to neutralize black support for the Populists and Republicans; and second, to keep whites from splitting their votes among three parties. Italians in New Orleans marched behind an Italian flag and cited their solidarity with the African Americans in protesting with the Populists against the amendment with a parade in New Orleans. The *Times Democrat* called the protesters "obnoxious," adding that "they interfere in American politics, and tell us what kind of a constitution, what system of laws, and what suffrage is acceptable to them as Italians."

Between 1892 and 1896, the Populists performed well in Louisiana elections and even ran a candidate for governor in the latter year. However, their policies appeared too progressive for the "solid South." By 1895, though, the national Republican Party had lost interest in blacks and exhibited more of a concern with the industrializing North and its emerging business opportunities. The Louisiana Democrats thus shifted their emphasis from economic to racial interests with their policy of disenfranchising blacks.

With the political atmosphere dictated by the Democratic Party and the state legislature firmly in the control of forces bent on disenfranchising African Americans, protests from the Populists and the Republicans echoed as the election of 1896 drew near. Seeking improvements in the state constitution, Populists and Republicans both agreed with revisions to the document, but not at the cost of alienating blacks—and Italians, for that matter—who could contribute not only politically to the region but also economically. The legislation Governor Foster proposed with regard to property qualification and educational requirements ultimately failed in the election of 1896, but Democrats took the calls for a constitutional convention and used them to oversee the creation of a document that enduringly disenfranchised African Americans in Louisiana.

The Populists hoped to garner the black vote in rural Louisiana, while at the same time reducing the racism exhibited by lower-class whites against the black rural population. Populists theorized that poor whites viewed their social status as one of an economic nature rather than of race and hoped that poor whites struggling to survive either as tenant or independent farmers would turn to their party to seek political redress for their depressed condition. Poor whites tested this theory by fusing with the Republican Party, the ranks of which also grew thanks to whites discontented with the Democratic Party who sought a just and equal society based on suffrage for all those citizens deserving of the right. In June 1896, the Louisiana legislature passed a new election law that accomplished part of the disenfranchisement goal. The Election Law of 1896 created assessors who acted as registrars and mandated that "persons applying to register should complete an application form in his own handwriting in the presence of an assessor or registrar." The registrations process effectively disenfranchised many black voters by demonstrating their inability to either write their names or "figure [their] age in terms of years, months, and days." New Orleans politico Martin

Behrman commented that the Election Law of 1896 "was intended to get as many white men on the rolls as possible and keep out as many Negroes as possible by giving the registrar of voters great authority." Once the Democrats perfected a method to disenfranchise blacks, Democratic leaders needed only a constitutional convention to statutorily restrict foreigners—namely Italians, blacks and those who could not own property—from voting. On this same day, the state legislature passed the Election Law of 1896 and also a resolution calling for a constitutional convention.

The Populists' collapse after 1896 dashed any hope of an equalizing factor in the South, despite the lack of cohesion with the whites in the Populist Party. Their survival would have demonstrated that poor whites and blacks in Louisiana stood united as a powerful political force. The white elite of Louisiana viewed anyone who believed in the equality of blacks, regardless of skin color, as an obstacle in the movement toward white cohesion. Political memories died hard in Louisiana, and Italians' alliances with the blacks in Louisiana could have spelled disaster for the Italians.

The constitutional convention of 1898 convened on February 8, 1898, and lasted until May 21 of that year. On the first day of the convention, the president of the august body, E.B. Kruttschnitt, stated that due to the "mass of corrupt and illiterate voters who have degraded our politics," if these voters were not disenfranchised, they would "jeopardize the integrity of the future government of the State of Louisiana."

One of the most powerful political organizations in the state, the New Orleans–based Choctaw Club, sought to use the convention to "put the negro out of politics" for good. Founded in March 1897 by future Democratic mayor of New Orleans Martin Behrman, the Choctaws considered themselves good Democrats, "organized against a Republican party." The Choctaws wanted to use the Italian vote to defeat the planters in predominantly black parishes. To accomplish this, they proposed a "grandfather clause" that essentially "permitted illiterate and propertyless whites to vote if their grandfather or father voted prior to January 1, 1867." A male who was twenty-one years of age and was a citizen of Louisiana and "of the United States, native-born or naturalized," could exercise his right to vote, provided "he shall be able to read and write, and shall demonstrate his ability to do so when he applies for registration." The person registering also had to take an oath "administered by the administration officer, or his deputy, written application therefore, in the English language or in his mother tongue."

In the event that an intended voter could not read or write, he could meet another voting requirement if, at the time of registration, he were "a bona fide owner of property assessed to him at a valuation of not less than three hundred dollars on the assessment roll of the current year in which he offers to register or on the roll of the previous year."

The final adoption of the 1898 Louisiana constitution stated, in pertinent part, that suffrage could be denied to "no male person who was on January 1, 1867, or to any date prior thereto, entitled to vote under the Constitution or statutes of any state of the United States, wherein he resided, and no son or grandson of any such person not less than twenty-one years of age at the date of adoption of this Constitution." Ensuring that no loopholes in the new suffrage amendments existed, Section 5, Article 198, provided that "in addition to the qualification above prescribed, [the voter must] have paid before the 31st day of December of each year, for the preceding year in which he offers to vote, a poll tax of one dollar per annum, to be used exclusively in aid of the public schools of the parish in which such tax shall have been collected; which tax is hereby imposed on every male resident of this state between the ages of twenty-one and sixty years." The constitution of 1898 also ensured that white Democratic officeholders would be appointed to positions in parishes where blacks were predominantly in the majority.

For the Italians, the Louisiana constitution of 1898 preserved their right to vote through a naturalization stipulation that covered all foreigners who were naturalized before the adoption of the present constitution. Despite their demonstrations of solidarity with blacks, local political bosses in New Orleans dominated the convention and had every intention of ensuring the foreigners' vote. For the ward bosses in the Crescent City, naturalizing and registering many poor and illiterate Italians served their interests and objectives of having a large, uneducated voting bloc. The remaining resolutions created a larger, more expansive white voting bloc.

Perhaps given the opportunity, whites again could attract the Italians to their side once the blacks lost any political voice. This created controversy that the Choctaw Club sought to make "the Dagoes citizens and disenfranchise the Negro, and God knows if there is any difference between them it is largely in the darkies' favor," as the Italians "are as black as the blackest Negro in existence."

On March 25, 1898, local newspapers announced that delegates at the constitutional convention had adopted a "suffrage clause." In essence, the Democrat-dominated constitutional convention "disenfranchised blacks and many poor white farmers who backed the Populist-Republican alliance." Simultaneously, the same delegates who rendered blacks ineffective as a voting bloc ensured the Italians that their right to vote would remain

Early growers and inspectors of bananas were Italians. Here is a scene depicted in the French Market of New Orleans in 1900. *Courtesy of the Library of Congress, Prints and Photographs Division.*

unscathed. This came with the assistance of the Democratic machine in New Orleans, which needed the Italian vote to hold on to its offices.

Although the new suffrage laws brought praise from the people of Louisiana and the South, elsewhere the new constitution brought scathing criticism, such as that "political chains were being forged for black men, the like of which have caused even South Carolina and Mississippi to blush with envy." The *Washington Bee* opined that Louisiana "had evils with which to contend in a large body of illiterate voters." The enactment of these provisions would certainly "cut down over two-thirds of the voting strength of the black voters in the state."

Chapter 7

Italians as Victims and Perpetrators

Should the facts really be as they have been reported to His Majesty's Government, the impression which this would create in the mind of the Government and upon public opinion in the Kingdom would be painful and disagreeable, because the outrage was an atrocious one, committed in the presence of many persons, and it is not conceivable that the guilty parties can not be identified.
—*Count G.C. Vinci, royal charges d'affaires of Italy, in correspondence to Secretary of State John Hay, July 25, 1899*

Observing the political maneuverings to disenfranchise blacks in Louisiana, Italians nearly lost any political voice because of their solidarity with African Americans. Had it not been for the local bosses in New Orleans who depended on the foreign vote to retain their powerful political positions, the Italians' right of suffrage would have been completely eliminated. The memory of the solidarity between blacks and Italians remained etched within the minds of Louisiana whites. The Italians' commonality with blacks made them targets of extra-legal violence. Furthermore, the nativist underpinnings that surfaced in the late nineteenth century stereotyped Italians and their alleged criminality. This period of Louisiana history played a rich part in what most Italians consider to be a blemish on their legacy.

STATISTICAL POPULATION FIGURES OF ST. CHARLES PARISH, 1880–1910

Year of Census	White Pop.	Black Pop.	Italian Pop.	Total Parish Pop.	Percentage of Italians v. Total Pop.
1880	1,401	5,746	4	7,161	0.05%
1890	1,986	5,751	0	7,737	----
1900	2,970	6,102	626	9,072	6.9%
1910	4,487	6,720	254	11,207	2.3%

Before the constitutional convention met in 1896, another lynching of Italians took place, this time in an outlying parish near New Orleans on August 8 of that year. Those killed included Lorenzo Saladino, charged with the murder of Jules Gueymard, a prominent St. Charles Parish businessman; Decino Sorcoro; and Angelo Mancuso.

Gueymard stood on the gallery of a Hahnville dock waiting for the arrival of a ship carrying some freight bound for his business. When the ship arrived, a shot rang out, killing Gueymard instantly. Authorities suspected Saladino of the murder because he and Gueymard were on opposite sides of a legal matter. When authorities searched Saladino's house, they found a shotgun that the suspect stated had not been fired in three months. One barrel showed evidence of firing. A "Mrs. Matorno," a woman living in his building, claimed Saladino came in late on the night of the murder and whispered under his breath, "I got him!" Sheriff Louis Ory saved the young Italian, as the crowd sought to lynch him that night.

Police officials arrested Sorcoro and Mancuso based on the suspicion of their commission of the murder of a Spanish yardman, Don Roxino, who worked on the Ashton Place Plantation near Boutte Station. The "old man" Roxino had been walking through the woods a week before the lynching when Sorcoro and Mancuso allegedly attacked him and then "overpowered him and he was prostrate on the ground as they beat him into insensibility."

Prior to the lynching, Sheriff Louis Ory posted extra guards at the parish jail, but on the following day, Ory removed the guards, leaving the shift jailer, Robert Peine, alone to guard the prisoners. One more day passed without incident, but on Saturday night, a large crowd gathered outside the jail. According to Judge Emile Rost and District Attorney Robert J. Perkins of St. Charles Parish, Peine stated, "On Saturday night, between 11 and 12 o'clock, the gate leading into the jail yard was broken, and the barred window looking into his [Peine's] room on the lower floor was forced open by prying out four iron bars and leaving an open passage."

A large group forced Peine to open the doors at gunpoint and threatened to kill the jailer unless he complied with their demands. The mob dragged Saladino, Sorcoro and Mancuso from their cells into the jail yard. Saladino, on his knees begging the crowd for mercy, stated, "I no killa Mr. Gueymard...I sleepa!" Saladino kept repeating himself, but to no avail. The crowd hanged him from an A frame in the jail shed, just a few yards from the jail doors. The command, "Haul him up, boys!" came from the crowd. Saladino stated to the lynch mob in his last words, "If there is a God, you alla will be punished." One of the mob yelled, "Hang the dago," and Saladino and the other two died a few minutes later. Judge Rost and District Attorney Perkins concluded their report with observations from alleged eyewitnesses who claimed they "knew nothing about the occurrence until the next morning," even though some of them lived less than a few feet from the jail yard where the lynching took place.

At the funeral two days later, blacks and Italians appeared together but left the graveside in extreme fear. Whites in St. Charles Parish feared this show of solidarity between the Italians and the blacks might serve as the initial stage in a revolt to seek revenge for the killings, but the uprising never materialized.

The Italian government sought to discover the truth, despite the lack of cooperation by local authorities. The events in St. Charles Parish threatened to cause another international incident, and white citizens expected Italy to demand reparations for the slain Italians. The editorials finally ceased their generalizations about Italians when they admitted, "While it is true there are a great many good and worthy Italians among us, it is equally true that there are a large number who are not desirable, being criminals who have fled their own country, or who have been forcibly deported by their government." Despite such conciliatory overtones, the editors of the newspaper opined, "For the presence of the worst element of these people in our country the Italian government is largely responsible." Demands against an indemnity to the Italian government became very vocal, and obligations to protect foreigners on American soil were questioned.

Baron Fava, still Italian ambassador to the United States in 1896, again stood at the forefront of the negotiations with the United States government. Fava, whose recall following the lynching of the eleven Italians in New Orleans five years before showed signs of an escalating conflict, compelled both local and national authorities to launch an investigation into the deaths of the three Italians in Hahnville. Fava wrote to Secretary of State Richard Olney informing him that the Italian government had learned of the murder and requesting of the secretary "to have the goodness to inform me what measures have been taken for the pursuit and trial of the guilty parties and for the repetition of such outrages against the safety of Italian citizens coming to settle in this country, and to whom the treaties in force assure the protection of these laws and these authorities." Fava firmly believed that the present case would be different from the previous incidents in New Orleans in 1891 and Colorado in 1895 and a satisfactory resolution for both sides could be amicably settled without the threat of war. Secretary Olney affirmed to the baron that a thorough investigation would be forthcoming.

The Italian consul of Louisiana, Charles Papini, conducted an investigation into the lynching and identified Sorcoro as one "Salvatore Arena," who came to the United States from Caccamo, Italy, in 1891, at the age of twenty-seven. Papini identified Mancuso as "Guiseppe Vontorelli," also from Caccamo, age forty-eight. The three men made their livings as farmers in the Hahnville area at the time and had associated with the deceased Spaniard Don Roxini. Papini also learned, more importantly, that Sheriff Ory was asleep during the lynching. Papini's efforts came to naught; Sheriff Ory's investigation lost urgency and motivation in discovering the truth regarding these murders.

In a communication to Fava, Olney diplomatically related the facts gathered by a special agent Olney sent to Hahnville to investigate. The agent noted that a grand jury assembled to investigate the matter and was "unable to ascertain the offenders. In their report to the court, they condemned in severe terms the outrage; but the district attorney who headed the proceedings failed to obtain any information, which could lead to the discovery and punishment of the guilty parties." Subsequently, no suspects were charged. The U.S. government, under Secretary Olney's auspices, denied the Italian nationality of the victims when he argued, "They were contributing nothing to the resources and wealth of Italy, were taking no part in her government, and were successfully evading the burdens of her military service." The secretary stressed the lack of evidence concerning the citizenship of the victims and the lack of responsibility on the part of the United States to provide any reparations for the loss of Italian citizens. Baron Fava later addressed Secretary Olney's suppositions when he opined that St. Charles did nothing to investigate the murders of the Italians. "No detective was put on the track of the assassins," Fava stressed, and "no attempt was made by police to discover them; and if the district attorney did not succeed in securing any information that could lead to the detection of the lynchers, this was due to the fact that no serious, courageous, or even partial attempt was made to that end." Fava warned Olney that unless the United States brought justice in this matter, violence against the Italians would continue without any legal consequences. Moreover, Fava strongly insinuated that the conclusions of the government's special agent validated the actions of a "defective" local justice system. Fava concluded, rather vehemently, that the three men killed in Hahnville "were not citizens of the United States" and "mere declaration of intention does not confer citizenship." Along with his points of contention, Fava professed that the Italian government would continue to persuade Secretary Olney into a favorable resolution of the matter.

Despite Papini's and Baron Fava's inability to identify the murderers, the Italian government proved that the three dead Italians had been subjects of King Humbert at the time of their deaths, and therefore, their families were entitled to an indemnity from the United States government. The government rendered $6,000 to each family, an amount much greater than that given to the families of the victims of the 1891 New Orleans lynching. An observer reasoned that the murder of Julian Gueymard "so foul naturally gave good reason" for the lynch mob to exact revenge on Sorcoro (Arena), Mancuso (Vontorelli) and Saladino. Attributing the crowd's reaction to Gueymard's murder as "passionate heat," this observer justified the lynching: "The white people up here are determined that the wanton murder by the Sicilians and Italians must stop, and they have adopted the severe method of lynching to teach them that they mean business."

THE TALLULAH MASSACRE

STATISTICAL POPULATION FIGURES OF MADISON PARISH

Year of Census	White Pop.	Black Pop.	Italian Pop.	Total Parish Pop.	Percentage of Italians v. Total Pop.
1880	1,261	12,645	2	13,906	0.014%
1890	931	13,204	---	14,135	---
1900	899	11,422	5	12,322	0.04%
1910	1,220	9,455	152	10,676	1.42%

In the summer of 1899, Italians in the tiny hamlet of Tallulah, Louisiana, in Madison Parish, experienced an event that has received minimal attention from historians. Tallulah was a small conclave of Italian farmers and storekeepers concentrated in the middle of the state. An Italian storekeeper named Joe DeFatta owned a herd of sheep that grazed behind his store on Front Street. The land buttressed that of a well-respected member in the community, Dr. J. Ford Hodge. Dr. Hodge continually warned DeFatta that his sheep were encroaching on his land, but DeFatta seemed to ignore those warnings, and the two argued frequently over the issue. The argument came to a head on the night of July 19, 1899, when Dr. Hodge shot and killed one of DeFatta's sheep. DeFatta went to see the doctor at his office the next morning and warned him against harming any of his other sheep. Hodge forced DeFatta to leave and thought the matter ended. That evening, as the doctor walked past DeFatta's store after dinner with another man, a Mr. Kauffman, DeFatta and one of his brothers, Charles, blurted an insult to Hodge. Charles then attacked Hodge, forcing him to the ground. As Hodge began to draw a pistol from his jacket, Joe DeFatta produced a double-barreled shotgun. He emptied both barrels into the doctor as he lay on the porch in front of the store, striking Dr. Hodge in the abdomen and the hands.

Another DeFatta brother, Frank, owned a shop just down Front Street from his brother's. Hearing the gunshots, Frank and two of his associates, Sy Deferroche and John Cereno, rushed toward Joe's store carrying shotguns and long knives. Sheriff Colman H. Lucas quickly subdued Frank, Deferroche and Cereno and brought them to the city jail. Joe and Charles DeFatta, meanwhile, barricaded themselves into their home just a few blocks from Joe's store. After a brief struggle, Sheriff C.H. Lucas arrested the two brothers. As he attempted to bring them to the city jail, a crowd estimated at over 250 citizens overpowered Lucas and his deputies and seized Joe and Charles DeFatta. The crowd took Joe and Charles into a nearby field, where the brothers blamed each other for the wounds Dr. Hodge sustained. The crowd, deaf to their protestations, hurriedly hanged the two brothers.

Worked into a bloody frenzy, the crowd turned their attention to the city jail. They broke in and seized Frank DeFatta, Deferroche and Cereno, forced them out of their cells and hanged them in the jailhouse yard. According to reports, "Not a shot was fired, and the crowd was orderly and quiet, but very determined." Unlike the other lynchings documented here, voices of reason attempted in vain to convince the frenzied crowd to spare the five men. The citizens exacting the extralegal justice would not listen to the pleas coming from other members of the crowd to spare the lives of the Italians. Previous accounts of the lynching of Italians portrayed the merciless actions of crowds devoid of any compassion. In the Tallulah case, the voice of reason finally spoke, though not persuasively enough to save the lives of the DeFattas, Deferroche and Cereno.

Even though the media attempted to raise the conscience of compassion for the Italians who were lynched in Tallulah, the investigation into the victims' pasts provided white justification for the extra-legal murders of the Italians. Two years before his death, Frank DeFatta was accused of shooting an African American who allegedly stole a watermelon from the front of his store. Although nothing could be proven, citizens of the small town strongly believed Frank committed the murder. A year prior to his death, Joe DeFatta allegedly shot and killed Pat McKenzie, a landing keeper, in cold blood. A jury later cleared him of the charge based on a technicality, but again, whispers of his guilt circulated among the local citizenry. The DeFattas often declared that they could do whatever they desired, becoming more brazen in their violence over time.

The repercussions from the Tallulah incident again caused an international incident between the United States and Italy. In this instance, Italy not only utilized the talents of a diplomat to negotiate with the United States but also became actively involved in the investigation itself. Count C.G. Vinci, charges d'affaires for the Italian government, noted to Robert Hay, the secretary of state under President William McKinley, that a grand jury in Madison Parish convened and investigated the incident but had been "wholly unable to discover the names of the perpetrators of the lynching." Italians who heard of the lynching, understandably, became enraged when they discovered that three of the lynching victims were not naturalized American citizens. The Italians expressed disgust at the lack of urgency on the part of local law enforcement to catch the perpetrators of murderous crimes against Italians. Italian newspapers commented that "this detestable form of administering justice is one of the customs of the Americans of the United States, and the indignant outcries of the civilized world have not been able to report it."

Count Vinci wrote strongly to Secretary Hay, impressing upon him that the United States government needed to expedite the investigation into the Tallulah lynching and prosecute those responsible for the murders. Secretary Hay reassured Count Vinci that he and the government would remain vigilant in their investigation. Vinci and his contemporaries were not so much concerned with the U.S. government but more with the Louisiana authorities who, in the past, had proven less than proactive when it came to investigating the murders of Italians. Diplomats such as Count Vinci and

Baron Fava knew the only way to receive satisfaction was to have Washington intervene with local authorities on behalf of the Italian government.

In reminding Italians of the inaction of the American government in past cases regarding the lynching of Italians, the Italian newspaper the *Fanulla* expressed "the hope that the Italian government will demand and insist upon an explanation of and satisfaction for the lynching." Rumors spread that Madison Parish officials strongly urged Italians to leave the parish, as their lives might understandably be in danger. Joe DeFino, brother-in-law to Joe DeFatta, made his way to Vicksburg, Mississippi, on a small boat after being warned that if Dr. Hodge died, so would DeFino. Sheriff Lucas stated that only two Italians remained in the parish, and they left Tallulah after hearing of the lynching of the other five Italians on July 20. Consul Nicholas Piazza, assigned to assist Papini with the investigation, expressed concern for his own safety after hearing some of the rumors, but Sheriff Lucas gave his guarantee that Piazza would be unmolested. Piazza began his investigation undisturbed.

Charles Papini, the Italian consul in New Orleans, launched an investigation into the rumors of the threats. Utilizing the investigative skills of Consul Piazza from nearby Vicksburg, Mississippi, and Chevalier Romano, gerant of the royal consulate, Piazza traveled to Tallulah for a full-fledged inquiry into the lynchings. Unlike the previous investigations, Louisiana authorities provided greater access to witnesses and evidence concerning the lynchings. Sheriff C.H. Lucas and Deputy Andrew Sevier, who stood in the crowd on that fateful night in mid-July, told the investigators almost identically that "had Joe and Frank DeFatta submitted quietly to arrest and had the other three Italians remained in Frank's store there would have been no lynching." Dr. Hodge, the intended victim of the DeFatta brothers and their friends who was still recovering from his wounds, said that he never sought out trouble with the DeFattas or the other Italian inhabitants of the city, except when the doctor had problems with the sheep walking on his porch the night before the altercation, making sleep impossible. Dr. Hodge complained to Frank DeFatta about the sheep but felt compelled to shoot two of the sheep, thus causing his own shooting and the lynching itself.

While investigations continued in Tallulah, Italy's experienced negotiator in conflicts past Baron Fava requested that the United States government keep him informed of any developments in the prosecutions that might occur as a result of the deaths of the five Italians. In response to his query, assistant acting U.S. secretary of state Alvey Adee wrote that he had received a copy of Sheriff Lucas's report with an attached addendum that stated that the guilty parties had not been apprehended and that the grand jury seated to determine those identities could not identify the perpetrators. Baron Fava then criticized Sheriff Lucas's dereliction of duty to discover the identities of the perpetrators, and having dealt with Louisiana authorities in two similar instances, Fava prepared for a protracted battle to bring the murderers to justice.

Although local authorities allowed Italian officials unprecedented access to witnesses and evidence in this investigation, from all indications the southern mindset toward the Italian immigrant remained unchanged. Papini, Romano and Piazza commended the town officials, including Pat Henry, mayor of Tallulah, for their hospitality and cooperation. The investigators issued a report, but the conclusions were of no consequence.

During the Italians' investigation, they discovered two black men who witnessed the lynchings up close and interviewed them away from Tallulah to protect their safety. One of them was killed in a mysterious incident once the word spread that he had divulged information about the lynching. The other, Joe Evans, who had worked for Joe DeFatta, named two other black men who could testify against the lynchers, if needed, and produced a list of nineteen men the four saw at the time of the lynching responsible for the murder of the five Italians. Among the nineteen, the main culprits furnished the rope, tied the knot and climbed the tree to make sure the rope did not slip from the tree branch.

As the events surrounding the lynching were made public, U.S. secretary of state Hay relayed the list of the five murdered Italians to Governor Murphy J. Foster. Fava then asked Secretary Hay what the government intended to do since Louisiana authorities had failed "to implicate anyone." Hay reminded Fava of the "dual nature" of the federal system, and Fava continued to demand an indemnity throughout the year 1900. Ultimately, President McKinley asked Congress for funds for relief to the deceased's families. Yet despite the payment of an indemnity, the Tallulah incident dissipated without the revelation of the identities of the murderers.

At the turn of the twentieth century, inhabitants of the South recognized that violence against Italians yielded no serious repercussions, at least from a legal standpoint. The lynching of eleven Italians in New Orleans in 1891 brought the United States and Italy to the brink of war and demonstrated the lengths to which each government would go to posture for its people. The aftermath of the 1896 lynching in Hahnville established a precedent that murderers of Italians would receive no punishment, and the 1899 execution of the five Italians in Tallulah firmly entrenched the belief in whites that the killing of Italians in Louisiana had no criminal penalties. As a signatory to the treaty with Italy in 1871 designed to protect Italians in the United States, both in person and property, the U.S. government ignored its obligations and sought to conclude these incidents with a rendering of indemnity. Rather than taking precautions to ensure that similar incidents would not occur in the future, the government's ineffectiveness in the investigation and prosecution of the guilty parties maintained a status quo and destined Italians to live in fear in Louisiana. Once considered as the "land of opportunity," to Italians the United States became a great threat to their lives and property. But despite the ominous atmosphere, Italian immigrants continued to call Louisiana their home.

For the most part, the Italian generations who grew up in the early part of the twentieth century were more apt to reject such a felonious mentality in favor of a more positive portrayal of Italians. Although such sentiment saw some popularity throughout Louisiana and the United States, the stigma of criminality still prevailed. Touted as a detriment to the Italian community, the Mafia generated fear among those who believed an underworld empire existed and contributed to the continuing "white" misunderstanding of the Italian population. Most Italians grew up with the notion that the Mafia was an embarrassment to the hardworking Italians in America, and they considered members of the alleged criminal organization to be "despicable" and "low-life."

In spite of the reactions of Italians who remembered the past discrimination and deaths of their compatriots, the attitudes of Americans and even native Louisianans slowly began to show more compassion, developing the relationships between themselves and the Italians. This alliance demonstrated itself in the fight against crime, no longer considered solely an ethnic problem. Whites and Italians realized that a societal difficulty could not be overcome unless they united in their mission to end crimes against the Italian people.

THE UNDERTAKER'S SON

One of the more publicized cases of violence against Italians in Louisiana history demonstrated that both whites and Italians could join to end the negative sentiment and violence and provided evidence of acceptance of Italians among the white population.

Italian headquarters, Madison Street, New Orleans, circa 1906. *Courtesy of the Library of Congress, Prints and Photographs Division.*

At 624 St. Philip Street between Royal and Chartres, Peter Lamana operated a funeral home for the most respected clientele of New Orleans. The funeral home also served as a residence that Lamana shared with his wife and their four children. On the evening of June 8, 1907, at 7:30 p.m., Mrs. Lamana called the children in for dinner. When the children and her husband sat down at the dinner table, she noticed that one of the children did not appear: little seven-year-old Walter Lamana. Lamana imposed on his neighbors to search for his son. At first, the neighbors and Lamana thought that Walter had crawled into one of the hearse wagons and fallen asleep, but when the neighborhood-wide search concluded with no sign of the little boy, his parents began to fear the worst.

After their search for young Walter failed to locate the boy within their neighborhood, Peter Lamana notified the police about his son's disappearance, and two detectives quickly arrived at the residence to begin an investigation. Throughout the night and into the next day, the search for the young boy continued, all to no avail. The search then expanded to include the outlying areas of the French Quarter and even as far away as the

The last known photograph of Walter Lamana, June 1907. *Courtesy of the* Times Picayune.

West End; Lamana believed the boy might have stowed away on a wagon to be near his uncle who lived there.

As the searches continued, a police officer came forward and related he had seen four children playing near Lake Pontchartrain at the West End at 4:00 p.m. but that none of them matched the missing boy's description. Lamana did not believe that his child had drowned. Thinking that the boy had been kidnapped rather than just wandered away, the police asked Lamana whether he had received any ransom demands for the boy's safe return.

Lamana denied (at first) that he had received any letters related to Walter's disappearance, but he did relate a story from two years previous when he thought he had become the target of thugs in his neighborhood. During the yellow fever epidemic of 1905, a loud banging noise at his front door had awakened Lamana. The undertaker thought someone wanted to engage his services, so he went out the doors leading to his front gallery and noticed a young black man standing behind a column. He whispered that he had a note for Lamana. Peter went downstairs and retrieved the note from the man. When asked where the note had come from, the black man stated he did not know. Lamana suspected at this time that the man who delivered the note had evil intentions for both him and his family and yelled at the messenger to leave immediately or he would shoot him.

On the morning of June 10, 1907, Peter Lamana received a letter written in Italian. The letter demanded money for the safe return of his son

Walter. Detailed instructions of how the money should be delivered to the kidnappers showed the determination and bravado of the kidnappers. The letter instructed Peter Lamana to travel on the road to Bogalusa with the ransom money. Lamana would meet a man who would collect the money, and then Walter would be returned unhurt. Peter Lamana stated that he would be willing to pay whatever it took to bring his son home unharmed.

On June 11, 1907, city leaders and the Italian citizens of New Orleans met at the Union Française Hall on Rampart Street at 7:00 p.m. The outpouring of grief and anger from the people at the gathering demonstrated the resolve of the attendees to discover the identity of Walter Lamana's kidnappers. It is interesting to note that also in attendance at the meeting that night were some of the very organizers of the lynching of the eleven Italians that took place at the Old Parish Prison on March 14, 1891. John C. Wickliffe, who had riled the crowd of upward of five thousand into such a frenzy before embarking on their murderous journey to the prison, sat on the podium with Edgar J. Ferrar, head of the Committee of the Fifty, to show their support of the Italians in New Orleans. Judge Philip J. Patorno, a lawyer and prominent citizen in the city, not to mention an influential Italian, stepped to the podium and stated:

> *The detective and police departments of New Orleans, as at present organized and managed, are inefficient to cope with the situation such that which now confronts the Italians. This is not because of any lack of numbers of other patrolmen or detectives, but because there are not two or three Italian detectives who are kept constantly employed in mixing with our people and ferreting out the criminals who are attempting to prey upon us.*

The gathering formed an Italian vigilance committee to look for the kidnapped Walter. Simultaneously, Peter Lamana led another search for his missing son in the backwoods of present-day Kenner, just nine miles north of New Orleans. Lamana asked that Sergeant William S. Coner of the Saratoga Street Station, Detective Ed Hollyland and Special Officer Walter Methe help him search for his son. During the search, the officers took turns attempting to gather information from Lamana concerning the note he had received the day before. The bereaved father remained silent concerning its contents.

Upon leaving the parish limits, Lamana, Coner, Hollyland and Methe met with two members of the Jefferson Parish Sheriff's Office, Sheriff Leo Marrero and Sergeant Fisher, along with two of their deputies. From there, the small posse made its way across the parish line into the adjoining parish of St. Charles. Although Lamana had not disclosed the contents of the letter to the detectives, he intimated that he was to meet a man on horseback. When the posse turned around and headed toward the small town of Kenner, a solitary horseman rode toward them. The detectives stopped and questioned the stranger. The man explained to the satisfaction of the detectives and Lamana that he had been out of town since morning. When the party finally reached the town of Kenner, they were going to take the train back to New Orleans.

Despite all their efforts that day, the Lamana posse was unable to discover the whereabouts of little Walter, nor did Lamana make any contact with the suspected kidnappers. When he returned to his residence, the distraught Lamana family members exhibited their frustration. Police began to suspect that since the young boy had been missing for so long, he may have met with foul play.

On the morning of June 12, 1907, after a long night's search, Peter Lamana could barely raise himself from his bed as exhaustion and grief took their toll on his physical well-being. A continued search of the neighborhood revealed the tale of a suspicious character who may have been a principal in the disappearance of the young Lamana. Tony Costa, a neighborhood ne'er-do-well, had not been seen in the neighborhood the day of Walter's disappearance. After word spread that Costa might have been involved with the young boy's disappearance, crowds gathered in the neighborhood bent on seeing Costa captured. Meanwhile, a rumor spread that the Lamana family would receive Walter's head later that night. Authorities organized a second search party for later that evening while other forces worked to bring the whole incident to a quick end.

On June 13, 1907, Italian leaders assisted police in rounding up suspects they thought might be involved with this crime, plus some new arrivals to the city. The police arrested Francesco Genova, a well-known importer; Sam Gernante; Giuseppe Cantosino; Lorenzo Giambelluca; Macaluso Chimo; Ignacio Campisciano; and Ignatio Caravelli. Influential members of the Italian community felt confident that the men arrested on that day were somehow responsible for the disappearance of little Walter Lamana. Genova complained to police that he held a great deal of wealth and did not want to be locked up with the others. Police ignored his request.

Acting mayor and councilman for the Fifth Ward James McCracken mandated that any questioning of the suspects would have to be done in the presence of the police. McCracken made it perfectly clear that there would be no extra-legal violence whatsoever once all suspects had been captured. The Italian committee met later on June 13 and adopted a measure pledging to support the authorities "with all the evidence they had in their possession and in the future." The Italian consul in New Orleans, Senior Scelsi, exhibited concern for the safety of the prisoners while they awaited arraignment. Based on previous history, he had good reason for concern.

Tony Costa, thought to be the mastermind of the plot, hid in plain sight at his residence on Clouet Street. On June 14, 1907, Judge Patorno and a police officer went to the Costa residence searching for the elusive fugitive. As the judge and the officer approached Costa's house, they saw a young girl sitting on the front steps. Within a blink of the eye, the young girl disappeared, and Judge Patorno and the police officer made a mad dash for the entrance to the house. When they ran upstairs, they discovered Costa lying in his bed. Not willing to take a chance that Costa hid a weapon under his pillow, Patorno held his weapon over Costa's heart and informed him of his arrest. Costa went peacefully but not before protesting his innocence. Police believed that Costa led the local criminal band in New Orleans. Sources later confirmed that Costa was seen with Walter at a local ice cream shop right before the boy's disappearance.

On June 15, 1907, Judge Patorno received a threatening letter. In this letter, the writer maintained that several powerful citizens in the city were responsible for the kidnapping of Walter Lamana. One sentence in the letter stated, "Do him like you done Politzi in the prison," referring to Manuel Polizzi, one of the eleven victims lynched on March 14, 1891. A mysterious affidavit then appeared pointing the finger at Costa as the planner of Walter Lamana's kidnapping. Even though the police released the other suspects, close surveillance followed them as they went about their daily routines, and police noticed they frequented their old haunts.

Peter Lamana received another letter that mentioned a man named Giovanni Barreca who possessed information about the kidnapping and where little Walter Lamana could be found. Lamana believed, after the receipt of this letter, that his son had been the victim of something sinister:

I shall never see my son again; I could not believe that men can be so cruel. I have lost all faith in my brothers and all that I can see ahead is years of suffering and misery and perhaps a maniac's cell. If I only knew that poor little Walter was dead my heart would not be so heavy but the feeling that he is in the hands at the black legs [Black Hand] *and perhaps being ill-treated and tortured is driving me mad.*

The search for Walter Lamana continued for another week without success. But near dawn on the morning of June 23, police and volunteers found the headless body of a young boy in St. Rose, St. Charles Parish, approximately fifteen miles from New Orleans. The coroner, Dr. J. O'Hara, viewed the body at the scene and determined that he had been strangled to death. Dr. O'Hara also noticed the trunk of the corpse had several broken bones. The police, searching the area more thoroughly, found the boy's head a short distance from his body. Trying to piece together the last minutes of the boy's life, the police theorized that one of the kidnappers silenced the boy through strangulation and then wrapped him in an old blanket. The murderer disemboweled the young boy's corpse and then threw the body parts in different sections of the woods. Tragically, the remains were later identified as those of Walter Lamana.

A young witness named Jennie Gariffo came forward and stated she saw little Walter the night of his kidnapping entering the cabin of Ignacio Campisciano. Campisciano knew the young girl saw something and later threatened her not to say anything or else. Police rearrested Campisciano and Giambelluca and added two more suspects to the cellblock: Leonardo Gebbia and Tony Gendusa, whom police brought to the parish prison on June 24, 1907. Gebbia and Gendusa did not resist arrest, and their passage through the streets drew no comments from the crowds. In addition, police brought Giuseppe Cantosino back to prison as well, along with Mrs. Campisciano as an accessory. Three new suspects fled the area once they learned of their impending arrest: Angelo Incarcetera, Francesco Luchesi and Stefano Monfre. Louisiana governor Newton C. Blanchard vowed to maintain order by placing the state militia on alert and reminding the populace that the suspects were innocent until proven guilty. Incidents such as the ones that plagued the state in 1891 and other successive years would not be tolerated.

By June 24, 1907, police felt they had arrested or soon would capture the persons responsible for Walter Lamana's kidnapping and murder: the Campiscianos, Gendusa, Costa, Leonardo and Nicolina Gebbia (brother and sister) and Angelo Monteleone, Leonardo Gebbia's brother-in-law. All were being held without any bond pending their arraignment. Those still at large included Francesco Luchesi, who, according to authorities, needed money to marry his girlfriend; Angelo Incarcetera, who held the child once he received him from Monfre, Luchesi and Tony Gendusa; Stefano Monfre, who had earlier eluded police in Cincinnati and Pittsburgh and whose wagon was used to transport Walter Lamana from New Orleans to St. Rose;

and Tony Gendusa himself, who, police alleged, wrote the ransom notes to Lamana. Police held eight persons in the Gretna jail for having taken part in the murder, while four were charged in absentia. When Peter Lamana received word concerning the incarceration of the suspects, he went to the parish prison to see if he could get a glance at the prisoners, specifically Campisciano. Lamana emphatically threatened that if the courts would not grant him justice, he would seek it on his own. Prison officials deemed this unwise and sent Lamana away.

One of the witnesses brought over from St. Charles Parish, Jennie Gariffo, stated in an interview:

> *On that Sunday morning about 5 o'clock, she was called by her father and told to get the coffee ready. There was not enough wood in the kitchen and she went out to cut some and then discovered the wagon in front of Campisciano's house. There were two men in the yard with Campisciano and one of these was holding a little boy by the hand. They were walking around the vegetable garden as if they were looking over the plants.*

Gariffo added that she saw a short man in a light gray suit with a straw hat walk into the door of the Campisciano cabin. Later on that day, she spotted another Italian man walk into the cabin. She then heard a little boy crying all night. The next morning, Gariffo did not hear the cries of the boy, and that afternoon she went up to the fence separating where she lived from the Campiscianos. Campisciano confronted her and asked, "What did you see?" The young girl replied she saw the little boy. Campisciano then warned her not to say anything to anyone concerning what she had witnessed over the previous two days.

Nicolina Gebbia, wife of Nicholas Gebbia, one of the alleged conspirators, volunteered to tell what she knew to the Italian vigilance committee. At the hotel where the committee held its meetings, Judge Patorno met the young woman, and she spoke for approximately an hour, not revealing more than authorities already knew. In later searches for evidence to corroborate Nicolina Gebbia's story, authorities in St. Charles Parish searched the Campisciano cabin and found a small hatchet with spots of blood still on the blade and a rope they surmised was used to strangle the boy. Police in St. Rose brought the evidence to Hahnville, where police examined it and ascertained its importance for their case. Police also discovered that Mrs. Campisciano acted as a guard and lookout while the little boy stayed in her cabin and her husband left to attend to other "business." Ms. Gebbia also alleged that Ignacio Campisciano hatched the plot to kidnap Walter Lamana and hold him for ransom, enlisting the others as accomplices to make some money.

On July 4, 1907, a grand jury indicted the suspects for the kidnapping and murder of Walter Lamana. Judge Prentice E. Edrington, of the district court for the Parish of St. Charles, formally appointed L. Robert Rivarde as the attorney for the accused murderers. Of all the suspects charged, Rivarde believed that Mrs. Campisciano only kept her silence out of fear of her husband and she should not be held as a murderer. Rivarde found Costa uncooperative when it came to relating his story.

The trial of the defendants in the kidnapping and murder of Walter Lamana began on July 15, 1907. The prosecution learned that Leonardo Gebbia wanted to turn state's evidence and testify against his co-defendants to take advantage of the slightest chance to save himself from the gallows. Gebbia told of a conversation that he heard between inmate Campisciano and a Joe di Pauella, who owned a farm adjacent to the Campisciano cabin. Gebbia stated:

> *The incident occurred when the two men were being prepared to be locked up. Di Pauella was walking at the side of Campisciano and when the guard turned for a few minutes, di Pauella fell to his knees in front of Campisciano and pleaded with him to keep an oath he made some weeks back. "For Christ's sake, don't give away on me," cried the poor fellow. Campisciano commanded di Pauella to be quiet and get on his feet for the guard was returning. "I'm not going to be hung" replied Campisciano. "My wife is going to get hanged or sent to the penitentiary…what will become of my two children? Will you take care of them both, will you be a father to them both and care for them just the same as I would if I were out of trouble?" Di Pauella said, "I swear!"*

Gebbia's testimony proved damning to the defense but especially to Tony Costa. Gebbia also testified that he saw Costa walk with the little boy to the corner of Royal and Dumaine Streets, place him in a covered wagon and drive off. Jennie Gariffo, the young girl who gave a statement to the police about her association with the Campiscianos, stated that she saw the covered wagon described by witnesses in the Campiscianos' yard and she saw two men lead little Walter Lamana into Campisciano's cabin.

On the second day of the trial, in a hushed courtroom, Mrs. Lamana, Walter's mother, approached the stand to give her testimony. In front of her on the prosecution's table sat the bloodstained clothing Walter wore on the day he was murdered. Overcome with insurmountable grief, she found it hard to contain her tears or her anger at the defendants as she shouted, "You are a bunch of murderers!" The outrage had no effect on the defendants, as they demonstrated no remorse. Mrs. Lamana stated that an old woman named "Mrs. Gebbia" came to her door on the Sunday morning after Walter disappeared and told her that the little boy had some ice cream at her house at approximately 5:00 p.m. on the afternoon of the kidnapping. Mrs. Gebbia told her "that the boy was in good health and had not been drowned as the mother suspected, but was in the hands of some bad men and it would be well to pay the money demanded." Mrs. Lamana noted that the Gebbia residence always received visitors at inappropriate hours of the day. On one occasion, she stated she saw a man with white shoes whom she could not identify, but she later gave the court the impression it was either Tony Gendusa or Tony Costa. Peter Lamana took the stand after his wife and gave incoherent testimony, still grieving over the death of his son. He stared at the bloody clothing still on the prosecution's table.

The evidence presented against the defendants was damning. Both sides then rested. The case went to the jury with Judge Edrington's charge: "The punishment for murder is death, but the jury may qualify its verdict by adding the word 'without capital punishment,' which would then confine the accused to the State Penitentiary at hard labor for the rest of their natural lives." Judge Edrington continued by explaining the rule of law as it related to "beyond a reasonable doubt," "circumstantial evidence" and the "rule of conspiracy." After the charges, the judge excused the jury to deliberate the evidence.

Twenty-four hours later, on July 19, 1907, the jury reached its verdict: all the defendants were guilty, but four were found "guilty without capital punishment." Newspapers around the country announced: KIDNAPPERS GUILTY; LYNCHING FEARED. Cries of "Lynch the Dagoes!" could be heard throughout the state. Governor Blanchard, who had already placed some state militia on alert, sent a detachment of them to Hahnville by a special train. Because of the presence of the troops, no one rose up and stormed the jail, despite the threats of several prominent New Orleans citizens to overwhelm the troops and kill the convicted. Although threats seemed credible, those making them lacked the nerve or motivation to follow through with them. The convicts served out their sentences in Angola State Penitentiary. Campisciano later confessed to the crime, stating that "after the refusal of Peter Lamana, the boy's father, to pay the $5,000 ransom," he had strangled the boy and thrown his body into a swamp near St. Rose.

The Lamana case produced more than just heartache for the grieving family and jail time for the heartless criminals. On a more positive and historical note, the case showed that Italians and non-Italians could join together to capture the perpetrators. Additionally, some of the prime movers of the investigation, Edgar Ferrar and John Wickliffe, had been deeply involved in the events leading to the 1891 lynching. Yet in this case, they moved very quickly to establish a mechanism to apprehend and prosecute the offenders. History does not record whether these men and others like them joined in the push to lynch those found guilty of Walter Lamana's death. Rather, the participation of these two men demonstrated some form of atonement for the reckless abandon in having the eleven Italians lynched sixteen years before.

A DEMON IN THE DEAD OF NIGHT

Huge slimy serpents writhe
Through murky pools;
A hurrying axman comes
With needful tools;
He quickly batters down
Resistant doors;
And from "the pit" the flame
Anew outpours.

Any reckoning of Italians in Louisiana would be incomplete without mentioning the brutal crimes that occurred in New Orleans and the surrounding areas between 1910 and 1919. The victims were predominantly Italian, and media outlets of the day (and law enforcement) placed credence in preposterous theories about whom the perpetrator may have been. The story of those dark days still generates fear and fascination for those who were introduced to it when they were younger or someone who hears of it presently for the first time. That is the story of the "Axman."

The terror supposedly began at 4:30 a.m. on May 23, 1918, when Jake Maggio awoke from a sound sleep because of moaning he heard through a thin plaster wall. As Jake arose to investigate, he awoke his brother Andrew, who was sleeping off a night of drunken revelry, having been called to service in General Pershing's army. Jake and Andrew then went next door to their

SCENE OF LATEST NEW ORLEANS MURDER

Joseph Maggio and his wife, from a photograph taken on their wedding day fifteen years ago, and the house in which they were killed while asleep in their bed.

The Maggio murder announcement that appeared in the New Orleans *Daily Picayune*, May 24, 1918. *Courtesy of the* Times Picayune.

brother's room, passed the kitchen and discovered a bottom panel of the kitchen door knocked out and the door opened. When the two entered their brother's bedroom, they found their brother Joseph and his wife, Catherine, lying on their bed in a pool of blood. Mrs. Maggio's head was split open with blood all over the floor and the bed. Captain John Drum, the first watch commander on the scene, found an empty strongbox and theorized that robbery was the motive. The police believed that the noise of removing a solid door panel would have produced more witnesses, but once they canvassed the area, no one reported having seen or heard anything. Mr. and Mrs. Maggio had been in the United States for approximately fifteen years and owned the corner grocery store below their dwelling at 4901 Magnolia Street in the Mid-City section of New Orleans.

Dr. Joseph O'Hara, coroner for Orleans Parish, determined during autopsy that "external and internal hemorrhages (of head and brain)" caused both the Maggios' deaths. Mrs. Maggio's first wound presented as "an incised wound beginning superficially under the right ear and entering deeply in center of thyroid cartilage, severing all vessels, nerves, and muscles, etc." Dr. O'Hara also determined that the killer used a razor on both victims to sever their throats, and a razor and ax were responsible for the deep cuts on their skulls.

Later that day, newly appointed detectives Theodore Obitz and Harry Dodson stumbled across a chalk message scrawled on the sidewalk two blocks away from the crime scene. The cryptic writing stated, "Mrs. Maggio is going to sit up tonight just like Mrs. Toney." Both of the detectives copied the exact words into their notes and placed them into the investigation file. What did the message mean? Who was "Mrs. Toney"?

Police brought in Andrew and Jake Maggio for questioning at the Seventh Precinct Police Station. The razor police found at the crime scene belonged to Andrew Maggio, and police questioned him incessantly despite his hungover state. Police later released the two. For the time being, the Maggios' murders would be classified as an isolated incident, even though there was a rumor spreading quickly throughout the city that the Mafia was involved. As time went on, authorities learned that the Maggios would be the first victims, and something more sinister was afoot.

In the early morning hours of June 28, thirty-five days after the Maggio murders, John Zanca, a baker, made his way to the grocery store of Louis Bessumer located at the corner of Dorgenois and LaHarpe Streets. Zanca knocked on the front door of the establishment and, having received no response, made his way to the side alley door to the living quarters that Bessumer shared with his wife. Zanca reacted with horror as he saw the bottom panel of the door missing. Bessumer answered the door with blood dripping down his face and stated to Zanca that the "Axman" had badly wounded his wife. When police arrived, they discovered a pool of blood where Mrs. Bessumer had lain and then dragged herself to the bedroom. In the bathroom, leaning against a wall of the bathtub, stood a bloody ax.

On June 29, 1918, police approached the Bessumer mystery from a new angle. Letters found written to Bessumer in German, Yiddish and Russian led police to believe that Louis Bessumer was the leader of a German spy ring. The letters discovered by the police brought federal authorities into the investigation and lent credibility to the assumption that Bessumer was a spy master for the Kaiser.

Police eventually deduced that the Bessumer attack had nothing to do with the Axman and was merely a domestic dispute gone awry. The Bessumer case became a media circus, and Louis Bessumer went so far as asking

Superintendent of Police Frank Mooney if he could be assigned to investigate his own case. Superintendent Mooney wasted no more time investigating the Bessumers and concluded that the present case had no connection with the Maggio murder. Because of the debacle, Superintendent Mooney demonstrated his frustration when he demoted two detectives assigned to the case, Thomas Balser and Michael Baradot, to the rank of patrolman.

While local authorities downplayed the Bessumer attack, the city remained free of attacks until the night of Monday, August 5, 1918. Mrs. Edward Schneider, nine months pregnant, lay in her bed alone because her husband worked nights. Her three children slept in the next room when, as she later related to police, a dark figure appeared over her and struck her in the head and face with a very hard object, knocking out her front teeth and rendering the young woman unconscious. Mrs. Schneider later regained consciousness at Charity Hospital and acted hysterically for fear she might lose her unborn child. Eventually, with the help of police, she regained her composure. The police later searched the Schneider residence and discovered an ax missing from the shed at the back of the house. Mrs. Schneider subsequently recovered from her wounds and later gave birth to a healthy baby girl.

The city remained quiet until August 10. On that date, police arrived at the grocery store at the corner of Tonti and Gravier Streets after receiving calls that something was wrong. When they arrived, police discovered the lifeless body of owner and barber Joseph Romano. Again, the police found no evidence suggesting the identity of the perpetrator, yet two witnesses in the room next to where Romano had slept heard what happened. Pauline Bruno, age eighteen, and her sister, Mary, age thirteen, lay in bed trying to sleep. Pauline stated to police:

> About 3 o'clock in the morning, I lay in bed awake. Then in the doorway leading to my uncle's room, I saw something I thought was a shadow. I thought at first I was dreaming. I realized then I was not for in the doorway was a tall heavyset man. He wore a dark suit [and] slouch Alpine hat. I screamed and the man ran out. Then my uncle staggered into my room and went to the parlor which joins it. He dropped into a chair, "something has happened, my head hurts, call for an ambulance." He fainted after that but was conscious after the police came.

Superintendent Mooney arrived on the scene and related, "I am of the belief that the murderer is a depraved criminal, a madman with no regard for human life."

Long before FBI profiles and the forming of its Behavioral Sciences Unit in Quantico, Virginia, in 1972, the evolution of DNA evidence and the refinement of fingerprinting, criminologists attempted to understand the criminal minds of even the most hardened perpetrators by utilizing the experience of law enforcement and the tools available at the time. A retired detective at the time of the Axman attacks, John D'Antonio (who also investigated the Lamana kidnapping), a respected and astute lawman, gave his impressions of the killer and, perhaps ironically, an early profile and subsequent victimological theories:

> *I am convinced the man is of a dual personality and it is very probable he is the man we tried so hard to get ten years ago when a series of axe and butcher knife murders was committed within a few months. My opinion is based on experience and a study of criminology. Students of crime have established that a criminal of the dual personality type may be a respectable law-abiding citizen when his normal self and suddenly the impulse to kill comes upon him and he must obey. It has been further proved that such fortunates remain normal for months, even years without being seized with the affliction. The Axman of ten years ago after being normal all these years might have broken out again…Criminals such as the one in question are on the order of "Jack the Ripper" who some years ago terrorized London. They are cunning and hard to catch. The police seldom run them down nor do they work at random. They have their plans well-laid before attacking a victim. "Jack the Ripper" was never caught. That his criminal work came to an end probably was because of his death…As in the cases of ten years ago, the recent ax murders appear to have been committed without motive, although practically all the victims were Italians, I do not believe the Black Hand had anything to do with any of them. I have never known the Black Hand to kill women, in fact, you could not get a Mafia agent to murder a woman under any circumstances.*

D'Antonio further believed that the assault on Mrs. Edward Schneider was part of the Axman attacks. In the earlier assaults D'Antonio mentioned, the aged detective had been intimately involved as an investigator years earlier and found some similarities with the present cases.

The attacks that D'Antonio included in his examination took place between 1910 and 1917. In the early morning hours of August 14, 1910, August Crutti, who owned a grocery store at the corner of Lesseps and Royal Streets, had just settled into bed with his wife at approximately midnight.

Crutti suffered from chronic indigestion, and that night in particular, this malady caused Crutti to awaken not more than a half hour after lying down. He got out of bed and walked into his backyard, hoping the night air would relieve his discomfort. He returned to bed a few minutes later and fell back to sleep. At 3:00 a.m., Mrs. Crutti awoke and discovered a dark figure standing over her with what appeared to be a meat cleaver in his hand. The figure demanded money. Mrs. Crutti handed over all the money the couple had available at the time. She then asked for her husband and shook him to turn him over. Mrs. Crutti was horrified to discover that her husband had been wounded, bleeding from deep gashes to his head. As Mr. Crutti tried to raise himself up in the bed to help his wife, the intruder struck Mr. Crutti again with the cleaver, more forcefully, and Crutti fell off the bed as a result of the blow's force. The mysterious attacker made his escape into the night. Crutti survived his wounds after a lengthy recuperation.

The stranger struck again just five weeks later, on September 21, with an attack on Mr. and Mrs. Joseph Risetto, who owned a corner grocery store at London and Tonti Avenues. At the time of the attack, Mr. Risetto's wounds were so severe that doctors thought he would not last the night. Eventually, the two would heal from their wounds and reunite in the hospital. Mrs. Risetto suffered lasting effects from her wound, leaving her paralyzed on the left side of her body and without her right eye. Still, the police had no leads, and the killer seemed incredibly elusive.

For over a year, the shadowy figure who had assaulted the Cruttis and the Risettos remained quiet. Then, on June 28, 1911, Joseph Davi and his wife were attacked in their sleep by an unknown assailant with a blunt instrument at 1:00 a.m. The assailant gained entry into the Davi residence located at 2425 Galvez Street through a window at the back of the house and made his way to the couple's bedroom. The intruder struck Mr. Davi over the head and fractured his skull. Mrs. Davi received cuts on her nose and hands. Joseph Davi later died as a result of the wounds he received that night. Mary Davi, although never able to positively identify her attacker and the man who killed her husband, stated that "she would devote the balance of her life to find the murderer or murderers of her husband." Subsequent to the death of Joseph Davi, the police arrested two suspects but later released them for lack of evidence.

Another attack took place the following year when, on May 16, 1912, Corporal George Duffy of the Fifth Precinct received a call from a Fred W. Stegelmayer, who resided at 4212 Villere Street. Stegelmayer heard gunshots coming from the barroom owned by Anthony J. Sciambra located at the corner of France and Villere Streets. Corporal Duffy proceeded to the Sciambra residence located behind the barroom and discovered the nude body of Anthony with gunshot wounds to the back and his wife, Johanna Sciambra, severely wounded and unconscious with a gunshot to the hip. Corporal Duffy attempted to question Mrs. Sciambra later when she could barely sustain consciousness, but she could not identify the assailant. Corporal Duffy, along with Chief Detective George Long, Officer Henry Sheffler and Patrolman Frank Williams, made a thorough search of the Sciambra residence and discovered two boxes stacked on top of each other below the kitchen window. At that time, police noticed that each of the neighborhoods affected were quiet enough for the assailant to commit his crimes undisturbed.

Dr. Joseph O'Hara's autopsy reports on the couple demonstrated gunshot wounds to Mr. Sciambra in the sternum and face, with "perforations of the bowel," causing massive internal bleeding. Additionally, Mrs. Sciambra suffered from a gunshot wound to the stomach that eventually caused her demise. Dr. O'Hara did not indicate through his viewing of the bodies or from his autopsy that anything but a revolver or pistol was used to commit the murders. Panic did not ensue, as in the future 1918 killings, with police viewing them as isolated incidents with the only common factor being that the grocers were Italian and their deaths caused by gunshot rather than an edged weapon.

The attacks stopped after the 1912 Sciambra murders until December 22, 1917, when a Mrs. Andollini awoke to find a dark figure standing on her husband's side of the bed. She screamed and then saw the figure strike her husband with a small hatchet. Once the intruder struck Mr. Andollini with the hatchet, he rushed into another room where the couple's sons, John and Salvadore, awoke to the sounds of their mother's screams. The intruder struck John in the head with the dull end of the hatchet and then struck Salvadore's left arm with the butt end of a pistol. This intruder, however, held closer to the pattern of future Axman attacks. According to police, the intruder chiseled out a door panel at the back of the dwelling and entered by reaching through and unlocking the door. The intruder left the hatchet near the kitchen door as he exited, the same way he entered the residence. Mary Andollini, the couple's sixteen-year-old daughter, only learned of the intruder when she heard her mother scream. The only link to the previous crimes came from the mode of assault and entrance. The Andollinis, sons and all, survived the attack.

Until D'Antonio mentioned the previous crimes, Superintendent Mooney had forgotten about the similarities completely. The retired detective did not know how close he would come to describing the killer's personality. The killer's escalation in violence and his boldness of entry signified an evolution in his methods.

In an effort to lighten the atmosphere surrounding the attacks, one business used the Axman as a means to draw people into its market. Its ad appeared on August 19, 1918, and stated, "The Axeman will appear in city on Saturday, August 24, and that he will ruthlessly use the Piggly-Wiggly ax to cut off the heads" of all high prices. Granted, the advertisement displayed bad taste, but New Orleanians relied on a sense of humor to allay their fears of the killer.

Subsequently, the Axman hysteria gripped the city as grown men held shotguns in their laps, sitting up in chairs to make sure their families remained protected. Eventually, though, the fear subsided temporarily, and the citizens celebrated the year-ending holidays, ringing in 1919 with much fanfare. Two months would pass in the new year before the Axman made his presence felt again.

Far from his normal stalking grounds, the murderer crossed the Mississippi River to the small principality of Gretna to exact his next victims. Charles Cortimiglia normally opened the doors to the grocery his wife owned at 5:00 a.m. every day. Hazel Jackson, a visitor stopping by on Sunday, March 9, 1919, noticed that the Cortimiglias did not answer their door when she knocked. Jackson went around to the side alley door and noticed that below the Cortimiglias' bedroom window was a chair. The window to their bedroom appeared to be opened, and when she walked to their back door, she noticed one of the door panels had been removed.

Law enforcement officials from New Orleans, Gretna and Jefferson Parish converged on the Cortimiglia residence located at the corner of Jefferson and Second Streets. The killer had murdered two-year-old Mary Cortimiglia first and then attacked the father and mother. Mrs. Cortimiglia cried for her deceased child as she lay mortally wounded in the hospital.

When Mrs. Cortimiglia regained consciousness, she identified the seventeen-year-old son of a business rival of Mr. Cortimiglia, Orlando Guagliardo Jr., as the assailant. "He did it," declared Mrs. Cortimiglia, "[he] is the man who hit me!" Orlando Guagliardo Sr., the thirty-seven-year-old father of the suspect, faced criminal charges of murder as well as assault when Mrs. Cortimiglia also identified him as an accomplice. When the police found the ax used on the Cortimiglias in the assault under the steps of the Cortimiglias' kitchen door, a bloody patch of Mrs. Cortimiglia's hair was still clinging to the blade. A Guagliardo descendant who related the story passed down through the family stated that Mrs. Cortimiglia used to work for Orlando Guagliardo Sr. and left to start her own business across the street from the Guagliardo establishment in an attempt to put him out of business. This new store, according to the Guagliardo descendant, was financed by the Black Hand, which previously had not been able to get the elder Guagliardo to buy certain supplies for his business from the group. For some reason, Mrs. Cortimiglia sought to eliminate, allegedly through the auspices of a Mafia front, a business rival by accusing him of the death of her husband and little girl.

Subsequent to the Cortimiglia attack, Superintendent Mooney gave a candid interview to the local newspapers. Mooney believed that the assaults committed between 1912 and 1918 were the work of one man (thanks to D'Antonio). Superintendent Mooney stated:

> *As these axe murders have grown in numbers, I have been forced to the belief that they are the work of a madman. I am convinced that the murders...are the work of an axe-wielding degenerate who has no robbery motive but who has taken small sums to throw the police off the track. I further believe...* [he] *is a sadist and that he crawls through the panel of the door, after going into the house, he opens the door. I have consulted several prominent persons who have made a study of crimes and criminals and most of them are of the opinion that it is the work of one man whose obsession is to hack people with an axe.*

Although Superintendent Mooney enlisted the help of criminologists, the mystery of whether the Axman acted alone puzzled police. The crime scene gave no indication as to whether the murderer had any accomplices. Mooney labeled the killer as a "degenerate maniac," having murdered a child with ice-cold sociopathy, and authorities dismissed the Mafia theory as it pertained to the attacks. According to the profile built by Detective D'Antonio and accepted lore, the Mafia did not murder women or children. With the Cortimiglia attack, a young child lay dead and the family devastated with the loss of that child. It is highly unlikely that the Mafia could have seen a child so young as a threat to business or identifying a potential killer. Terror throughout the area intensified as no one appeared safe from the Axman's blade.

On March 16, 1919, a local newspaper received a letter dated "Hell" and signed "The Axman," openly taunting the police. The letter was addressed to "Esteemed Mortal" and stated that the writer was not human "but a spirit and full demon from hottest hell." The unknown author continued, "When I see fit I shall come forth and claim other victims...I shall leave a clue except my bloody axe besmeared with the blood and brains of whom I am sent below to keep me company." Despite all the supernatural connotations, the person calling himself the Axman offered a brief respite from his nocturnal slaughter. "Now to be exact," the letter continued, "at 12:15 o'clock (earthly time) on next Tuesday night, I am going to pass over New Orleans. In my infinite mercy, I am going to make a proposition to people." The author of the letter stated that if the city would play jazz at the time he mentioned, he would pass over without any attacks. If everyone in the city did not comply, they "will get the ax."

Examination of this note in present-day terms reveals that since the author never related details of the crimes attributable to the Axman, it would be hard to believe the killer and the author of the letter were one and the same. In earlier letters of this caliber, a written document containing details of the murder that had not been publicized would convince authorities that the author of the letter had committed the attacks.

The "Mrs. Toney" message left on the sidewalk two blocks from the Maggio murder in 1918 and the letter written to the newspaper in 1919 drew comparisons to a case earlier mentioned by Detective D'Antonio in his assessment of the killings that occurred between August and November 1888: those of the serial killer known as "Jack the Ripper."

Jack the Ripper claimed five victims, all prostitutes or "unfortunates," in the Whitechapel District of London in the fall of 1888. The Axman mimicked several aspects of his predecessor when the former scrawled the "Mrs. Toney" message near the crime scene of the Maggio murder. This seemed eerily reminiscent of a message that the Whitechapel murderer left inside a doorway at 19 Ghoulston Street, London, after the "double event": the murder of two prostitutes on the same night, Elizabeth Stride and Catherine Eddowes, on September 30, 1888. The message said, "The Juwes are the Men that will not be blamed for nothing." Even then, only supposition could be used to speculate what the murderer meant. However, serial killers, including the Axman, seek the notoriety that accompanies their brutality and sometimes unspeakable offenses against their fellow human beings. The desire to acknowledge their crimes is a behavior that denotes a feeling of superiority over the authorities.

The individual responsible for the letter to the newspaper followed his mentor's example. Although the crimes were no less brutal, the Axman played on the fears of those he considered prey to accomplish whatever objective he desired. Modeling himself after the world's most famous serial killer, authorities speculated as to the depths that the murderer would reach before either his capture or death would end the reign of terror. In demanding the city play endless jazz so he might pass over and not claim any victims that evening, and the reaction of the city to the request, the murderer confirmed that he controlled the very essence of New Orleans. While he continued the assaults, he would eventually gain total domination of the denizens, paralyzing them with fear. On the other hand, continued execution of his ruse could subsequently lead to his capture and authorities, and the people of New Orleans desperately hoped he would eventually be caught.

After the receipt of the letter claiming to be that of the Axman's hand, an Italian pianist named Joseph John Davilla composed "The Mysterious Axeman's Jazz," or "Papa Don't Scare Me." Other musicians of the time reviewed the composition and deemed it comical—a serious embarrassment set against the backdrop of the most violent murders in the city's history. New Orleanians prepared for their night of jazz, hoping to defer any further attacks. The Whitechapel murderer never requested such a compliant event but would have been proud of his pupil's coercive powers.

On March 16, 1919, Jefferson Parish courts officially arraigned the Guagliardos for the attacks on the Cortimiglias and the murder of their little girl, Mary. With the only arrest made in the Axman case, the court set their trial for May, and according to the police, they had their murderers. Orlando Guagliardo Jr. received a death sentence, while his father, Orlando Guagliardo Sr., received a life sentence. Mrs. Cortimiglia came forward after the convictions and confessed she had accused the wrong men of the murder of her daughter. She stated that "Saint Joseph, the patron saint of all Italians, had appeared to her in a dream and instructed her to tell the truth and to beg her neighbors' forgiveness." The Guagliardos walked out of the Gretna jail free men. As a result of the treatment that the Guagliardos received from residents around Jefferson Parish and in an attempt to put the incident behind them, they changed their name to "Jordano."

Exactly as the Axman demanded, at 12:15 a.m. on March 19, 1919, "many Orleanians took the axman letter, printed in the *Times Picayune* Sunday, seriously, and that scores of others who did not take it seriously, found in it inspiration for house parties with jazz music having a prominent place in the program." A local newspaper also printed a cartoon entitled "The Witching Hour," with whole families participating in the playing of jazz and a woman perceived as being the mother standing at the darkened window, keeping vigil and waiting for a nighttime visitor. "Cafes all over town were jammed. Neighbors gathered in homes to 'jazz it up.' Midnight found the city alive with the canned music of the period. Inner player pianos and phonographs, in the levee and negro districts, banjoes, guitars, and mandolins strummed the jazziest kind of music." The Axman granted the city a reprieve from his nocturnal visits.

THE WITCHING HOUR—12:15 A.M.

"Witching Hour" cartoon that appeared in the *Daily Picayune*, depicting one of the killer's wishes. *Courtesy of the* Times Picayune.

The Axman's bloodlust continued on August 3, 1919, when Sarah Laumann, a nineteen-year-old girl, felt something heavy crash down on her head in the dead of night. Laumann later recovered and remembered scaring the perpetrator out of her bedroom. "Ms. Laumann was not the proprietor of a grocery; she was not Italian; her assailant had not entered by a door panel, but had used a window."

At 1:40 a.m. on October 27, 1919, the Axman allegedly claimed his last victim. Jefferson Parish sheriff's deputy Ben Corcoran was walking home from a long shift at the station when eleven-year-old Rosie Pepitone ran out into the street and screamed that her father had sustained wounds that left him bleeding from his head. When Deputy Corcoran entered the Pepitone residence located at 3842 Ulloa Street, Mrs. Esther Pepitone met him immediately and stated, "It looks like the Axman was here and murdered Mike." Deputy Corcoran went into the Pepitones' bedroom and saw Mike Pepitone lying on the bed, barely conscious, with a large gaping wound on the left side of his head and the bedsheet stained with fresh blood. An ambulance rushed Mike Pepitone to Charity Hospital, where he later succumbed to his wounds. Dr. E.J. Bergier, who performed the autopsy, determined that Pepitone sustained a crushed skull in several places, and the killer in this instance used a heavy iron bar with a bolt on one end to inflict Pepitone's wounds. Police found the murder weapon at the crime scene and matched it to the wounds the victim sustained. Other than the excited utterances of Mrs. Pepitone, police found no other evidence that connected the previous attacks with that of Mike Pepitone.

The killer entered the Pepitone residence by breaking two panes of glass in the window of the dining room adjoining the sleeping quarters of the couple. The murderer (or, in this case, the murderers, according to the testimony of the victim's wife) passed his hand through the shutters and unlocked the window to gain entry into the house. Authorities suspected that the murder of Mike Pepitone was a revenge killing disguised as the remains of a serial killer's wake. In 1910, Peter Pepitone, Mike's father, had shot and killed Charles Di Christina, a rival grocer, at the corner of Calliope and Howard Streets. Pepitone's father stood trial, and the jury found him guilty of murder and sentenced him to twenty years in the state penitentiary, but he received a pardon after serving only three years. Police theorized that Mike Pepitone knew something of his father's plans to kill a rival. But why wait almost ten years to seek revenge through an elaborate ruse?

During a police interview, Mrs. Pepitone stated that when she awoke, "she saw the form of a tall slim man and a smaller man, much heavier going through a rear room." The police were baffled that six of the Pepitones' children slept in the room where the attack occurred and not one of them awoke; Mrs. Pepitone was the only one in the household who witnessed anything. The circumstances surrounding the Pepitone attack did not follow the normal pattern of the Axman killer. The method of entry differed, as well as the chosen weapon of assault and the fact that the intruder did not remove the door panels. Instead of the victim's garden ax, a heavy iron bar with a bolt at its end signified the killer's attempt not only to seriously injure the victim but also to cause the most amount of damage in a short period of time. Additionally, the killer left Mrs. Pepitone and the other children alone, much unlike the previous attacks where women and children also fell victim to the ax swing.

The Axman's reign of terror abruptly ended in the New Orleans area after the Pepitone killing. Questions remained as to the identity of this elusive killer and his motives. Was he a psycho killer, as characterized by Superintendent Mooney and Detective D'Antonio, taking a hint from Jack the Ripper on how to remain undetected? Or was he a demon, as he stated in his letter to the newspaper, yearning to return to his native "Tartarus," where the climate better suited his physiology? No one knew for sure, and historians speculated for years afterward about the true identity of Louisiana's first serial murderer.

Although the case of the Axman would dissipate on the local level, the tale resurfaced half a continent away and caused much excitement in New Orleans. Newspaper headlines in December 1921 reported that a woman named Mrs. Esther Albano shot and killed a man named Joseph Mumfre in her California home. Mrs. Albano declared that the man demanded money from her, and when she refused to pay, he became violent and she had to defend herself and her children living in the house with her. Police later identified Mrs. Albano as the former Mrs. Mike Pepitone, wife of the last Axman victim in New Orleans. Since being named in connection with the case, Mrs. Albano has not received fair treatment throughout history. In a recent interview with an Albano family member who chose to remain anonymous, a more dignified portrait of Esther Albano emerges rather than the accepted unflattering version local historians intimated for over ninety years.

The relative's story begins in late 1921, when Esther Pepitone traveled to Los Angeles, California, to attend her niece's wedding. While there, she met Angelo Albano, also from New Orleans, and they married a short time after their meeting. On October 27, 1921, Mrs. Albano reported her husband missing. She alerted relatives in New Orleans, who came out to California to search for her missing husband, but to no avail. Angelo Albano had disappeared without a trace.

Subsequent to Angelo Albano's disappearance, at the Albano residence in California, the family received a visitor who told them where the family could locate the missing uncle and offered to give them the information for a price. Mrs. Albano told police that "[Joseph] Mumfre repeatedly threatened to kill Angelo Albano if the latter did not give him money." She claimed Mumfre had murdered her present husband, but Mrs. Albano gave no indications that Mumfre had murdered her first husband, Mike Pepitone. Mumfre (now using the alias "M.G. Leone") came to Mrs. Albano's home on December 5, 1921, and "demanded that she give him $500 and attempted to kill her when she refused." The relative continued, "She was worried, she had a bunch of kids in the house and this guy was threatening her and she had to take care of it." Los Angeles Police subsequently arrested Mrs. Albano and held her until her trial in April 1922. After a four-month jail stay, a jury found her not guilty of the murder of Joseph Mumfre (M.G. Leone).

Over the last ninety years, historians and investigators alike have speculated as to the connection between Mrs. Albano and the Axman murders in New Orleans. Additionally, there have been numerous articles on the subject that attempt to besmirch the reputations of Italian ancestors surrounding the case, especially that of Mrs. Albano. The relative of Mrs. Albano interviewed took exception to the way history has depicted his ancestor. "She was a great woman, a great woman," he said. A genuinely caring individual, Esther

Albano was always concerned with her family, she worked hard to make her business run smoothly and she fed people free of charge during the Great Depression when they had no money. Esther Albano never spoke ill of anyone. After careful examination of available research on the subject and a credible consultation with family members, it would seem the judgment passed on Mrs. Albano is undeserved.

From a historical standpoint, if one examines the history of the individual whom many historians claim murdered under the moniker of the "Axman," he seems more of an ordinary hoodlum than a criminally deranged mastermind avoiding detection throughout the course of his reign. According to police, "Joseph Mumfre" had a long criminal history and alleged affiliations with the local underworld in New Orleans. In extensive examinations of available primary sources, "Joseph Mumfre" did not exist. A shady character known to have associated with various underworld circles, "Joseph Monfre," however, warrants closer examination.

There are certain inconsistencies with Monfre's alleged involvement with the Axman murders. He came to the attention of police in 1908, when he and an accomplice, Albert Panieollo, blew up an Italian grocery owned by a Mr. Graffignini at Cleveland Avenue and Claiborne Street. Panieollo entered Angola while Monfre waited for an appeal of his conviction. On November 4, 1908, the Louisiana State Supreme Court denied Monfre's appeal stemming from a conviction involving the bombing; Monfre entered Angola to serve his sentence on January 13, 1909. On June 2, 1915, Monfre enjoyed a brief period of freedom when the state paroled him, but he "returned to Angola after a violation of his parole" on July 10, 1916. The entry next to his name in the Angola Registry showed Monfre owed a year, a month and eight days for his violation of parole, and authorities delayed his release date until August 21, 1923. The records indicate that Monfre served the full time without any further releases for good behavior. History then lost track of this alleged killer after his release from Angola State Penitentiary. Unless he flew, like many believed the Axman capable, Monfre's involvement with the Axman murders can be discounted at this point.

The Axman makes for a timeless tale of horror in the strange-but-true realm. It is doubtful that the identity of the killer, being so far removed in time, will ever be discovered. But amateur sleuths and professional historians certainly can entertain themselves with the likely thought of discovering some document or photo in someone's attic that would definitively point to a suspect.

"Bloody Tangipahoa"

Statistical Population Figures for Tangipahoa Parish

Year of Census	White Pop.	Black Pop.	Italian Pop.	Total Parish Pop.	Percentage of Italians v. Total Pop.
1880	5,608	4,104	7	9,638	0.07%
1890	7,943	4,698	8	12,655	0.06
1900	12,248	5,375	97	17,625	0.5%
1910	15,170	9,135	1,621	29,160	5.5%

Just a short distance from the urban growth of New Orleans, Tangipahoa Parish began as a conglomeration of several parishes as part of the short-lived West Florida republic in 1869. Its picturesque pines and sleepy attitude provided a welcome change for the Italians seeking an escape from the poverty and overcrowding of the city. Despite the serene atmosphere of this small woodland community, Tangipahoa and the cities within the parish still saw their share of racially and politically motivated violence.

Starting at the end of Reconstruction, the lynching of blacks became a common practice as the Knights of the White Camellia, the violent arm of the Louisiana Democratic Party (with a similar ideology to the Ku Klux Klan), lynched unsuspecting blacks in an attempt to regain Democratic control over the area. One of the Knights' leaders in the area, Judge Thomas C.W. Ellis, despised Republican rule and vowed to rid the state of anti-Democratic influences, including blacks, immigrants or any other denizens who sought to maintain Republican domination of the state. This laid the foundation for later discrimination against the Italians settled in the area.

The earliest Italian immigrants to the area first journeyed to the small settlement of Independence, Louisiana, in 1890. A successful farm owner engaged in the raising of strawberries hired an Italian family to work as laborers in that year. Subsequently, more Italian families traveled to the area. They began to thrive, and within ten years, they convinced others in Sicily to make the journey to Tangipahoa Parish. Instead of Italians migrating out of the area at the end of respective growing seasons such as sugar cane and strawberry, they set down permanent roots. The Italian population grew from 8 in 1890 to more than 1,621 in 1910.

The antagonism against Italians first occurred in February 1908, when lumber mills in the Kentwood area kept Italians on the payroll while laying

When Italians made their way to St. Tammany Parish for the strawberry-growing season, they established roots in the parish and raised families there. This cemetery signified their willingness to move their families to better accommodations and work. *Courtesy of the Library of Congress, Prints and Photographs Division.*

off white employees. The companies running the mills justified their actions because the Italians worked harder and displayed more dedication to their jobs than the native whites who worked at the mills. This action created resentment among the native population of Tangipahoa and caused anti-Italian sentiment throughout the parish. A sheriff and thirty of his deputies stood at the ready due to the open threats to Italian families in the Kentwood area. Sheriff John Saal stated he would conduct an investigation before prosecuting the perpetrators of the threats. Law enforcement officials' strong stances were enhanced thanks to the reinforcement of state militia deployed to Kentwood from nearby Amite by Governor Newton C. Blanchard. Mill management tried to quell the Italians' fears, assuring them, as Italian families crowded the train platform in McComb City, Louisiana, bound for New Orleans, that "they were in no danger, that the soldiers and deputies would protect them, but the efforts of the gentlemen went for naught."

On March 1, 1908, Charles Pittaro, an Italian merchant living in the Kentwood area, received a letter from a city resident ordering Pittaro and his family to pack and leave his home before any danger befell them. The troops Governor Blanchard sent in, Company I of the Louisiana State Militia, arrested six men in connection with the threats, and the matter dissipated. Governor Blanchard continued to garrison troops in Kentwood to protect the Italian citizens.

Tangipahoa Parish remained quiet for over two months until July 22, 1908, when an Italian, Nick Tesitora, allegedly shot and wounded Deputy Sheriff Alex Watson in the small town of Natalbany, just a few miles from Kentwood. With no provocation, according to eyewitnesses, Tesitora fired at Watson from a shanty near the Illinois Central Railroad. Deputy Watson, severely wounded, returned fire and forced Tesitora to flee into the woods surrounding the town. Watson picked up Tesitora's trail until he found himself back in a general store in the middle of the town. Watson and Tesitora again exchanged gunfire until more deputies made their way into the store and forced the suspect to surrender. Deputies took Tesitora into custody. Watson later died from his wounds.

On July 23, 1908, posses of lawmen pursued three Italian brothers, Joe, George and Tony Liambisi, as a result of the alleged wounding of Walter Simmons, a millworker in Natalbany. The incident started as a common fistfight between an "American" youth and an Italian one in a local barroom. The young Italian happened to be the younger brother of the Liambisis. Simmons pulled for the American youth, while Joe Liambisi took up for his brother. The younger Liambisi got the better of the exchange. The other Liambisis, George and Tony, jumped into the fight and began pummeling the young American. Simmons saw this and took up his young champion's cause. George Liambisi brandished a revolver, and Simmons ran toward the door. George fired three times; all three rounds hit their mark, and Simmons fell to the floor, mortally wounded. George and Tony fled the scene, and the police arrested Joe when they arrived.

Simmons came from a well-respected family in Magnolia, Mississippi, and "was very popular among the Americans in this section of the parish." The search for his killer demanded expediency. Sheriff Saal hastened to Natalbany with several deputies, and once he arrived, he questioned Joe Liambisi at length. Joe Liambisi offered to act as a guide and interpreter for the posse to where he suspected his brothers to be hiding. Sheriff Saal accepted Liambisi's offer, and along with Liambisi and seven other deputies, the posse made their way to the town of Independence, where a small Italian settlement thrived. As the posse arrived, the little village roused.

Joe Liambisi stated he had made a mistake and led the posse to another dwelling just a short distance away. When Liambisi and Saal knocked, Joe Anzalone, the owner, opened the door with a loaded shotgun cradled in his arms. Liambisi asked Anzalone in Italian whether he would allow the deputies to search his home for the fugitive Liambisis. Anzalone opened fire, missing the sheriff and his deputies. This time, they returned fire and wounded Anzalone in the left arm and chest. Another man, Vincent Loscanto, rushed from the cabin with a shotgun, and one of the deputies took aim, fired and caught Loscanto in the legs. After a brief respite, Sheriff Saal organized his men into different groups to head in different directions to search for the two Liambisis. In Tickfaw, a few miles to the west of Natalbany, deputies encountered resistance while searching a house. Rumors quickly spread throughout Tangipahoa Parish about Italians committing random acts of violence on "American" populations, and mobs gathered to lynch prisoners already incarcerated. Tangipahoa Parish officials quickly dispelled those rumors.

Sheriff Saal learned on July 23, 1908, that Walter Simmons died as a result of his wounds. Saal took precautions to keep Joe Liambisi safe. The search for George and Tony Liambisi intensified, as they now faced murder charges instead of assault. On that same night, unknown assailants bombed an Italian grocery store. Even though no one sustained injuries as a result of the blast, Governor Blanchard ordered a small detachment of National Guardsmen to the area in the hopes that any further violence might be quelled. As a result of the intensification of violence, "forty Italians from Natalbany arrived in the city [New Orleans] yesterday morning…as they declare they will not go back to Tangipahoa."

The National Guard remained in Kentwood and sought to pacify the local population bent on mob justice as the Kentwood Vigilance Committee, formed after the shooting death of Walter Simmons, issued a proclamation wherein the Italians "were ordered to leave town under pain of death." Italians took the warning seriously and vacated the small town, leaving only half their original population of two hundred. Judge Tom Ellis recounted the events leading to the deployment of militia in Kentwood in his diary: "Trouble in Natalbany with Italians, Man named Jno. Simms [Walter Simmons] was of Magnolia killed by a Dago. State troops sent up to Hammond, when a Dago home was dynamited." As with the Hennessy case, the St. Charles lynching and the lynching in Tallulah, the Italian consulate felt it necessary to become involved and launched an investigation into the events affecting the Italians in Kentwood and Natalbany.

Confrontations concerning "Americans" and Italians in the Tangipahoa area continued despite local and state vigilance to prevent any further bloodshed. After the Watson/Tesitora shootout, Italians in Natalbany and their opponents exhibited uneasiness; both sides stood prepared to attack each other at the slightest provocation.

Vice Consul Geralamo Maroni traveled to Natalbany to address the concerns of the Italians there and assure them of their safety, but clearly the Italian government would not intervene on their behalf as in the past. The events of the previous months quieted, and eventually, on July 27, 1908, the governor recalled the troops. Tangipahoa Parish would stay calm—for a short time.

The reason for the negative sentiment toward Italians in Tangipahoa Parish can be attributed to their work ethic and desire to provide for their families. In turn, they provided economic competition to whites in the area. If it had not been for the actions of the state's highest executive and some quick-thinking law enforcement officers within the parish, another incident of the magnitude of the New Orleans lynching might have materialized and forced an all-out conflict between the Americans and the Italians.

Six for One

The strawberry harvest for the year 1921 broke several records for its abundance. Banks in Tangipahoa Parish held the proceeds of that season's

An Italian grower picking strawberries in a field near Hammond, Louisiana, 1939. *Courtesy of the Library of Congress, Prints and Photographs Division.*

Independence Bank. On May 8, 1921, six men from New Orleans attempted to rob the bank through the back in the yard of Dallas Calmes. *Courtesy of the author.*

profits. In places like Independence, the local bank seemed a likely target for robbery: it offered a rich score, an easy getaway and unlikely detection. During the age of Prohibition, thousands made millions without much toil smuggling liquor. Two aspiring bootleggers, Roy Leona and Joseph Giglio, traveled from New York to New Orleans to seek their fortunes in the illegal liquor trade and looked to robbing banks to gain a stake. The two met an alleged underworld figure named Vito Girogio, who informed the two men that the bank in Independence would be an easy score. Leona and Giglio then met their future fellow conspirators, Natale Deamore, Joseph Rini, Joseph Bocchio and Andrea Lamantia. Together, they met at Deamore's garage on Tulane Avenue to plan the robbery. On May 6, 1921, the six men left New Orleans and headed toward Independence for what they thought would be a large and easy payday.

Upon their arrival in the small town, the six men scouted their intended target and examined all escape routes. They also watched for any routines the bank employees exhibited and memorized their movements to synchronize their timing. After "casing" the bank, the six men decided that evening or the lightless hours of morning would be their best opportunity to rob the bank. The men proceeded to the house of a friend, where they planned to spend the night. As they discussed their plans for midnight of May 8, a young man living in the house overheard them.

In the early morning hours of May 8, 1921, Mrs. Dallas Calmes, the wife of a hotel and restaurant proprietor in Independence, heard a noise outside her back door. The Calmeses' back fence buttressed the wall leading to the inside of the Independence bank. Mrs. Calmes awoke her husband and alerted him to the noises she heard outside their back door. Mr. Calmes immediately grabbed his .32-caliber pistol and ran to the back door. When he opened the door, a fusillade of gunshots rang out, mortally wounding Mr. Calmes. Mrs. Calmes desperately pulled his bullet-riddled body back into the house. The assailants then made their escape.

Roy Calmes, Dallas's nephew, heard the shots and ran to his uncle's side. Roy then ran to the home of a neighbor, Tom Candiotto, and asked to borrow Candiotto's new 1921 Ford to pursue the robbers. Roy Calmes and three other men headed off into the night after the six Italians.

As Roy Calmes and his three pursuers made their way down the lonely country road near Independence, they came across a car parked on the side of the road. A young boy and an older man appeared to be working on the engine. Suspicious of the stopped automobile, Calmes and the others stopped and asked if they could help. The man and the boy stated they needed no assistance. Calmes drove on for a brief moment but then became suspicious of the stalled vehicle and devised a plan to discover the identities of the mysterious men in the car. Calmes and the other men with him turned their vehicle on its side, blocking the road. Just as Calmes surmised, the "bandit" car stopped in the middle of the road to avoid crashing into Calmes's overturned vehicle. Roy Calmes appeared from behind the overturned vehicle and yelled, "Halt!" Gunfire erupted from the stopped automobile, and then the vehicle emptied, its inhabitants running into the nearby woods. A later account of the incident recalled: "In the chase that followed, several hundred men took part. They found where the fugitives had dropped a lot of cartridges and a shotgun, and finally capturing four of them…Bloodhounds were obtained from the state penitentiary but did not arrive until after the capture of the six referred to had been effected." Police eventually arrested Natale Deamore, Joseph Bocchio, Joseph Rini, Andrew (née Andrea) Lamantia, Roy Leona and Joseph Giglio. Police also arrested Nick D'Amore and Joe Deamore, both fourteen years of age, as accessories to the unsuccessful attempted robbery of the bank and the murder of Dallas Calmes. Because of concerns for the prisoners' safety, local Tangipahoa authorities transported the prisoners to Magnolia, Mississippi, and then to New Orleans.

Little did the police know that the Calmes murder may have been related to a double homicide that occurred in New Orleans two days prior to the Independence incident. Dominick di Giovanni and Joseph Gaeto drove down Tupelo Street at 2:30 a.m. and stopped in front of the home of Leonardo Cipollo. As soon as the car halted, gunshots rang out. Within moments, di Giovanni and Gaeto lay dead from "buckshot and slugs." Letters seized from one of the six suspects who attempted to rob the Independence Bank, Joseph Giglio, revealed an address, 983 St. Maurice Avenue. Assistant district attorney for Orleans Parish Thomas Craven went to the address, where he spoke with Tony Corollo and discovered that Leonardo Cipollo regularly received mail at the St. Maurice address, even though he lived two blocks away.

Authorities suspected a connection between the two murdered men and the Italian gang responsible for the trouble in Independence. It appeared the gang had planned the double homicide in conjunction with the crimes they committed in the piney woods of Louisiana. Cipollo fled the area when the police sought him in connection with the captured Italians. Later searches revealed that he took his family with him.

In an effort to positively identify the suspects, police brought in nine-year-old Joe Liatta, who, while eating cupcakes and accepting coin change from doting detectives and patrolmen, identified six men as the perpetrators he saw in the car the night of the Independence crime. Steadily, the members of the gang appeared to break down. Natale Deamore stated that the other members of the gang forced him to go along at gunpoint as an unwilling party to their actions. When the other prisoners heard that Deamore confessed, they became enraged at his betrayal. But the story of little Joe Liatta, as far as it concerned the police, sealed the fate of the six Italians he identified. Young Liatta stated the six men approached his father, Joseph Liatta, and his uncle, Natale Giamaldo, to join them in their plans. Liatta and Giamaldo at first refused the demand, and the boy heard the men say "they were going to the bank to get some money." The boy did not flinch in giving his rendition of the events, and police expressed no doubts about the sincerity of his identifications.

Meanwhile, New Orleans police and Assistant District Attorney Craven searched Cipollo's residence in an attempt to find not only a link between the two events but also Cipollo's affiliation in the hierarchy of an underworld organization in the Crescent City. Along with several barrels of homemade wine and cognac, authorities found four license plates from cars reported stolen two weeks prior to the search, .32- and .38-caliber ammunition, one shotgun, two shotgun cases and a plentiful supply of the ammunition that police identified as the type used in the di Giovanni and Gaeto murders. A more in-depth examination of the Cipollo household yielded two pieces of addressed correspondence to Andrew Lamantia and Joseph Rini, plus some business papers that included thousands of dollars in checks Cipollo wrote. Tony Corollo later elaborated that Cipollo came to his store on many occasions to pick up telegrams and mail addressed to Cipollo from men identified as the "Independence gang," specifically Joseph Rini.

During the search of Cipollo's residence, Natale Deamore stated from his jail cell that he wanted to talk to Assistant District Attorney Craven. After two days of isolation, Deamore finally broke. When Craven arrived at the Ninth Precinct police station, he forced the prisoner to identify the others involved in the Calmes murder. Rini and Deamore faced each other in the interrogation room of the police station, and "Rini's lips moved in a low mutter of Italian oaths. His eyes glared at Damore [sic]. His manacled hands shook with passion as the fingers clutched and writhed yearningly. He was led from the room protesting that Deamore lied." Rini continued his protestations and subsequently lunged for Deamore, grabbing him by the throat and cursing him in Italian. Two detectives standing nearby grabbed Rini just in time to save Deamore from asphyxiation.

Police subsequently arrested the two strawberry farmers, Liatta and Giamaldo, after Deamore identified them as the men who harbored the gang in Independence when they arrived from New Orleans. Liatta and Giamaldo identified Deamore as one of the more anxious of the group, characterizing him as impatient and almost bloodthirsty. Liatta later identified Roy Leona as another member of the robbery party. It turned out that he and his son, "little Joe," the youngster whom police had earlier showered with candy and coins to entice his identification of the suspects, were unwilling participants in the getaway, with Rini and Leona threatening the family if they did not comply with the gang's demands. They threatened the elder Liatta not to reveal their plans to anyone for the whole day prior to the attempted bank robbery and the Calmes murder. Liatta and his son pretended to have car trouble the night of the crime, and Roy Calmes encountered the "old man" and the child on the road from Independence in the search for the men who killed his uncle.

On May 11, 1921, after several days of surveillance, police followed Cipollo from the law offices of George J. Gulotti to a grocery store near the scene of the di Giovanni and Gaeto murders a few days earlier. Detectives Joseph Cassard and George Reyer found Leonardo Cipollo hiding behind a barrel on the second story of the establishment. The detectives then took him to the Seventh Precinct police station at Napoleon Avenue and Magazine Street. There, Detectives Cassard and Reyer and Assistant District Attorney Craven questioned their suspect.

When queried concerning the double murder, Cipollo stated that he and his wife stood next to the death car when an "unknown" assailant (or assailants) fired into the vehicle and riddled the unsuspecting men with gunshots. Cipollo repeatedly uttered, "Bom! Bom! I hit the grass. I ran away," and told his interrogators that he had no idea where his wife went after the shooting. After relating his rendition of the facts, police arrested Tony Corollo, the owner of the grocery store where Cipollo hid for three days without detection. Although small facets of his story changed slightly, Cipollo steadfastly maintained his innocence in the attempted robbery of the Independence Farmers and Merchants Bank, the murder of Dallas Calmes and the murders of Dominick di Giovanni and Joseph Gaeto. Later in the interrogations, Cipollo related so many different variations of his story that authorities sought other eyewitnesses for reliable accounts of the incidents in question.

The prosecution's star witness, little Joe Liatta, awoke on May 12, 1921, to discover that he was in the protection of the Tangipahoa Parish sheriff, who stated that if the boy was returned to his family, "he would share the same fate as Walter Lamana." Joseph Liatta, the elder, placed himself in harm's way as he identified Joseph Giglio as one of the gang members. The elder Liatta and his son claimed that Giglio and Leona stopped at their residence and demanded they guide the robbers out of Independence after the attempted robbery and Calmes's murder.

Authorities in New Orleans subsequently received a letter from James Corrigan, a bereaved father from Toledo, Ohio. His son, George, allegedly died at the hands of Joseph Rini, one of the suspects in the murder of Dallas Calmes. The elder Corrigan wrote that on May 24, 1920, several Italian men murdered his son while he was visiting a woman named "Mrs. McDonald," whose home was used as a haven for underworld types in the Toledo area. Witnesses identified the man who actually pulled the trigger as Joseph "Scratch" Rini. Additionally, police discovered that Roy Leona and Joseph Giglio had previously traveled throughout Louisiana and Mississippi robbing banks and making $50,000 for their illegal efforts.

Several of the suspects, including those named here, attempted to gain their freedom through habeas corpus motions, but jurists denied them.

The prisoners remained separated in jails in St. Bernard, Tangipahoa and Orleans Parishes. A grand jury in Amite City, Louisiana, in Tangipahoa Parish, indicted nine suspects for the murder of Dallas Calmes and the attempted robbery of the Farmers and Merchants Bank in Independence: Joseph Rini, Andrew Lamantia, Roy Leona, Joseph Giglio, Natale Deamore, Frank Pisciotto, Natale Giamaldi and Petro Liatta. Leonardo Cipollo sat in the St. Bernard Parish jail for what authorities termed "safekeeping." The Amite grand jury did not indict Leo Prestia or his father, Anthony Prestia, owners of the automobile used on May 9, 1921.

Just when the police felt they had convictions ensured with the cooperation of one of the conspirators, Natale Deamore fell silent. Police hoped Deamore would divulge the details surrounding di Giovanni's and Gaeto's murders, as well as the attempted bank robbery and murder in Independence. Despite his silence, police felt confident they could make the connection between the Tupelo Street murders and the actions of the gang while in Independence.

Assistant District Attorney Thomas Craven discovered the reason behind Deamore's sudden reluctance to serve as an informer: Cipollo and two others began planning Deamore's murder when they discovered he had approached authorities about lessening the charges against him in exchange for his cooperation. Craven hypothesized that Deamore decided to take his chances with the courts rather than face certain death at the hands of his fellow suspects. Because of his reluctance to continue, Deamore faced the same charges as the other eight suspects.

As the suspects awaited their trial, certain citizens advocated the organization of a vigilance committee under the leadership of Cono Puglisi, editor of the Italian-language newspaper *L'Italo Americano*, to "assist authorities in arresting and prosecuting those whom he [Puglisi] referred to as his 'desperate countrymen.'" Such advocacy demonstrated that Italians in the region had grown tired of the typical Italian stereotype of violence rooted in ethnicity. The vigilance committee, in theory, demonstrated good intentions, as had the many formed before it, and if organized properly, it could have served to heighten public awareness with the skills of law enforcement. When the judicial system displayed what it considered due process and the outcome enraged the populace, the moniker "vigilance" could transform the most docile personality into a brutish avenger. In this atmosphere, though, police remained confident that the evidence they had against the suspects would convince a grand jury to bring an indictment for the crimes charged. Eventually, a Tangipahoa grand jury returned a true bill charging the men to stand trial in front of the Honorable Robert S. Ellis on June 13, 1921, in the Twenty-fifth Judicial Court for the Parish of Tangipahoa.

The first trial of the eight suspects resulted in a conviction of six and an acquittal of two. The jury sentenced Rini, Lamantia, Leona, Bocchio and Deamore to hang for their parts in the murder of Dallas Calmes. Cipollo and the rest of the defendants walked away free men, but the police held Cipollo over for his expected arraignment in the murders of di Giovanni and Gaeto, even though police were unclear about the extent of his involvement.

Over the next three years, the defendants filed several appeals that proved unsuccessful, and the sentences were to be carried out as adjudicated by the court. The day before the execution was to take place, on May 8, 1924, Mrs. Natale Deamore arrived at the courthouse adjoining the jail to visit her husband for what would be the last time. Her two children—Domica, twelve, and Santo, eleven—accompanied her. During the excitement of the day's preparations, Mrs. Deamore recognized Mrs. Calmes, Dallas Calmes's widow, standing in a hallway speaking with Lem Bowden, the sheriff of Tangipahoa Parish. Mrs. Deamore suggested that the two young children approach Mrs. Calmes and ask her to intervene on behalf of their father. Mrs. Calmes told the children she could do nothing, but the children's plea touched her. Mrs. Deamore then approached Mrs. Calmes and begged for her forgiveness, pleading with her to intervene on behalf of her husband. Mrs. Calmes responded, "I do forgive your husband, but remember I am going out to my husband's grave at once. You know what I went through and now you must face the same. I forgive your husband, but you must suffer as I have." With that, the conversation ended.

Mrs. Deamore and her two children then turned toward the jail to visit her husband. Arriving near the jailer's post, they found Sam and William Rini, Joseph Rini's father and brother, and Dominick Giglio, Joseph Giglio's nephew, waiting to tell their relatives goodbye. An eyewitness described the scene between the Deamores: "For fifteen minutes husband, wife, and children talked between passionate outbursts of sobbing. There were tears in the eyes of soldiers and deputies as they turned from the cell, Mrs. Deamore and her two children walked slowly down the stairs, and out of the jail past the gallows by which Deamore will be hanged by the neck until dead at noon Friday."

Governor John Parker called troops of the 108th Cavalry of the Louisiana National Guard to ensure the hangings took place as scheduled without any unexpected rioting. Eyewitnesses remarked that Italians in the town went about their business as they normally would have on any other workday. Occasionally, an Italian citizen would pass a small assemblage of men discussing the day's events without focusing on the execution of the six men to occur later that day. An Italian man interviewed that morning stated, "I did not understand how it could be right for six men to die for the killing of one, but now I understand everybody in a conspiracy is equally guilty." Newspaper reporters approached Italians in Amite for further commentary on the trial; they, too, agreed with the court's verdict and refused to challenge it.

The tolling of the bell at the Amite town hall at noon on May 9, 1924, marked the commencement of the death walk scheduled for that day. The night before, a priest from the local church had given the prisoners their last rites. Authorities planned to execute the condemned men two at a time: Deamore and Bocchio; Giglio and Lamantia; and, finally, Leona and Rini. Crowds gathered outside the gates of the Amite jail yard in an attempt to hear or see anything. Troops of the 108th Cavalry patrolled the area outside the jail in anticipation of a riot. No disturbance materialized, and the area remained quiet throughout the executions. The drama took place inside as the hour grew near.

Fathers Munichia and Martinez from the local Catholic parish led the procession from the cells. Deamore and Leona walked solemnly behind them, followed by the jail guards. Sheriff Bowden changed the order of the prisoners without any notification to anyone, including the condemned. The men made their way to the top of the thirteenth step, were escorted over the trapdoors and had their legs and hands bound and black hoods placed over their heads. When the doors dropped, Deamore and Leona died instantly, their necks breaking as their full weight tested the strength of the noose. Andrea Lamantia, hearing the mechanisms of the scaffold release, attempted to take his own life by stabbing himself repeatedly in the chest. He did not die but bled profusely. Nothing would cheat the hangman that day, and the executions continued. Lamantia and Bocchio, again led by the priests who gave them the last rites, walked up the steps to the gallows. As Bocchio reached the last step, he fainted. The executioners assisted him to the trapdoor and carried out the sentence of the court. As the last pair, Giglio and Rini, walked to the gallows, Rini blurted out, "I hope you devils will be satisfied. You butchered four, and now you are going to butcher two more." Although no one at the time could be sure which of the condemned men stated it, one of them said, "Governor Parker made it a total of seventeen Italians lynched and hanged."

The Italian people recognized that the despised, stereotypical criminal elements of their particular ethnic group would eventually pay for their crimes. Additionally, it reinforced the ability for the native white population and the Italians to unite to dispense righteous justice. The justice system worked in both the Lamana and Calmes cases to the point where the anti-Italian sentiment waned in favor of a logical and judicious resolution. These episodes laid the foundation for the acceptance of Italians as true Americans.

Chapter 8

Conclusion

The Italian experience in Louisiana history served as an example of naiveté in an age of political manipulation, economic turmoil and vigilantism. Whites of Louisiana accepted the Italian immigrants with open arms—provided they could contribute to the maintenance of white power within the state while contributing to the economic recovery of the area. The Italians strove to create better lives for themselves and their families, but due to their lack of racial prejudice toward blacks, they encountered an onslaught of racial discrimination and hatred that they did not understand.

Subsequently, white natives adjusted to the inclusion of Italians within the cultural, social and even political spheres of Louisiana, and the accomplishments of Italians in these domains cannot be overstated. Several looked to make their fortunes, while others sought to improve the lives of those less fortunate. Inadvertently, some of these individuals left indelible marks of the Italian legacy in Louisiana. Angelo Socola became known as the "Father of the Rice Industry" and managed a large rice mill prior to the Civil War. Santo Oteri began an import business that would later become the United Fruit Company in 1868. Dr. Felix Formento Jr. received degrees from Louisiana College and the University of Toronto and served the Confederacy at the Louisiana Hospital in Richmond, Virginia, where he successfully experimented in skin grafting. Antonio Monteleone, a descendant of royal blood from Sicily, made his way to New Orleans, where he opened a shoemaking shop. By 1886, Monteleone had saved enough money to buy a small hotel at the corner of Royal and Iberville Streets. The hotel remains in existence and bears the name of its original Italian owner; it is considered one of the most luxurious hotels in the world.

One of the most celebrated Italians in the Crescent City arrived as manna from heaven itself. Born Saint Angelo Lodigiano, Mother Xavier Cabrini, as she came to be known, founded the Missionary Sisters of the Sacred Heart of Jesus around 1880 and sought permission from Pope Leo XIII to organize missions in the Far East. Instead, the pontiff recommended she travel to the United States and set up missions for Italians who immigrated here and were languishing in poverty. Mother Cabrini subsequently concentrated her efforts on the poor Italians of Chicago, St. Louis and, finally, New Orleans, where her influence may still be felt by Italians in the area. In 1895, she and her missionaries managed to establish stations in Metairie Ridge, Harvey and Kenner, where a great deal of Italians had settled near the end of the nineteenth century. This was not an easy task, especially in Kenner, where children were generally needed to work on the farms and had no time for formal education. But Mother Cabrini and her missionaries worked to educate the children and the adults of the region.

Mother Cabrini visited several schools in New Orleans that her

order founded to help the Italian immigrants to raise themselves from the slums and their impoverished condition. These visitations took place regularly, and when Mother Cabrini visited New Orleans in 1904, she was pleased to see that the orphanage on St. Philip Street still held to the mission of "elevation and education of the Italian immigrants along the lines of good American citizenship and true Christianity." In the yellow fever epidemic of 1905, Mother Cabrini urged her sisters to make the sick more comfortable. She continued her work for many years thereafter, and she oversaw the

Mother Francesca Cabrini (1850–1917), founder of numerous Italian benevolent associations to assist the Italian immigrants to the United States with their transition to being American.

funding, building and dedication of orphanages and schools in Louisiana and other parts of the nation with equal vigor and determination. Mother Cabrini sought for Italians to preserve their cultural individuality while at the same time endeavoring to embrace their new homeland. Mother Cabrini died on December 23, 1917, and was canonized on July 7, 1946, by Pope Pius XII as the "Patroness of Emigrants." Several schools still possess her name, including Xavier Cabrini High School located on Esplanade Avenue in New Orleans. On that campus, the room where Mother Cabrini stayed during her numerous visits to New Orleans is still preserved for the public to view.

And, of course, there are the Italian heroes of music. Dominick "Nick" La Rocca has been touted as the father of modern jazz, and who could forget the musical stylings and "swinging" persona of Louis Prima. These men produced pride within the Italian community of New Orleans, both at the time of their popularity and even today.

In the political realm, Italians made their presence known, first as a voting bloc and then as voices of the people in general. The complicated and often distrustful world of Louisiana politics seemed like a sphere in which the Italians and their descendants would not take part, especially since past experience with those machinations had proved dangerous. But instead of shying away, politics seemed to attract those Italians who could use their positions to help their people and prove that not all Italians were part of some criminal conspiracy.

With the rise of Huey Pierce Long in Louisiana during the 1920s and 1930s, he used his country logic to win the hearts and minds of the working class in Louisiana. Long used questionable tactics to win political support for the various reforms he wanted to pass through the Louisiana state legislature. The "Kingfish" surrounded himself with men of a similar mindset and a similar socioeconomic background as his own. It was in this atmosphere that Robert S. Maestri, the first Italian American mayor of New Orleans, became part of Long's inner circle. Maestri aligned himself with the "Kingfish," and even after Long's death, Maestri reaped the benefits from his close association with Long.

Maestri made his fortune by expanding his father's already successful furniture store and investing the profits in real estate. Many believed that the younger Maestri made money through investments in gambling and prostitution, but most maintained he had above-average business acumen. Not as eloquent or politically savvy as most politicians, and certainly nothing like the political mastermind Huey Long, Maestri did not necessarily want political power for himself. Rather, he wanted Long's programs to be implemented in New Orleans. Maestri, therefore, concerned himself with fighting the political organization known as the "Old Regulars," a political machine that had held the balance of power in New Orleans since the beginning of the twentieth century. If Long were to make any progress in the city, the Old Regulars had to be defeated, and Maestri served as Long's general on this battlefield.

In 1935, the battles between the "Longites"—steadfast supporters of the Kingfish—and the Old Regulars continued. But in September of that year, an assassin's bullet claimed Long's life. T. Semmes Walmsley, then the embattled mayor of New Orleans, and the Old Regulars may have believed they could regain control of the city from Long's grasp, but the mayor steadily angered the political machine that supported him so faithfully, and it now shifted its support to Long candidates. Since Long's death, the Kingfish's influence seemed eerily intensified, and his legacy with the people still held strength. Support for Walmsley dried up within the Old Regulars, and he found himself alone, a sheep in a room full of wolves. On May 9, 1936, Walmsley resigned, and he gave his farewell address on June 20, 1936.

Due to some secret political maneuvering and a need to eliminate Old Regular Walmsley, Maestri won the office unopposed when the only Republican candidate withdrew from the race. Maestri "became mayor of New Orleans without a single ballot cast in his favor." To enrich his power and patronage, the Louisiana state legislature passed an amendment so that Maestri would not have to face any opponents in the mayoral election of 1938. This solidified Mayor Maestri's control of the city's chief executive office, and he served six years without opposition.

Mayor Maestri's first term saw many improvements in the economic standing of the city. He convinced local banks to lend money to the city at a lower interest rate than normal. Maestri also took the time to make daily tours of New Orleans with engineer and head of the City Development Panning Board (and Governor Leche's father-in-law) Hampton Reynolds to make sure that street projects were being maintained and that locations that needed his attention were assessed. Mayor Maestri also made himself available to the working people of the city. After completing his tours with Reynolds, Maestri would arrive at his office at 10:00 a.m. to listen to the concerns of the citizens who visited him at city hall. Despite a few accusations that he had enhanced his personal fortune through the office of mayor, his first term pleased most of the city's denizens. His second term, however, beginning in 1942, saw Maestri as more reclusive from the people, and he devoted more and more of his time in managing the Old Regulars and the

Longites. Maestri neglected the city as it reverted to the corruption of the past.

In spite of his attention to factional fidelity, Maestri did pave the way for other Italian American politicians and public servants to gain success within that realm. Most notable were Joseph and Clarence Giarusso, the former a city councilman and the latter a superintendent of police; Pascal Calogero, the first Italian American on the Louisiana Supreme Court; and Congressman Steve Scalise, who has demonstrated leadership and resilience in the United States Senate during some of the most trying times in recent American history.

The accomplishments of Italians in Louisiana reflected their upbringing and the importance of their heritage. When first coming to Louisiana, the Italians did not isolate themselves from other ethnic groups. Perhaps this, along with their lack of prejudice for blacks, or anyone else for that matter, contributed to their racial isolation by whites. The descendants of Italians who made their way to this part of the country heeded the wisdom of their parents and grandparents when assimilating into white society. "Son, do the best you can and don't worry about it…Get an education!" stated Angelo Spinato Jr.'s father. Spinato learned valuable lessons growing up during the Great Depression as an Italian in New Orleans, especially when dealing with people of other ethnicities. Where he grew up in Mid-City New Orleans, Spinato made friends from many ethnicities. He recalled a run-in with a young Irish boy. "We had one fight," remarked Spinato, "and then we were friends for life. That's the thing about Italians: once you get to know us, you have a friend for life," and those friends appreciated the Italians more. Spinato later served his country in the Battle of the Bulge and some of the most horrendous fighting in the European Theater during World War II.

Donald Gennaro, whose parents and grandparents ran a restaurant/barroom at the corner of Felicity and Rampart Streets, lived in a neighborhood with blacks and Italians, and "it was peaceful to coexist with the blacks and Italians all in the neighborhood. They had barrooms and shoemaker shops" and worked there alongside the Italians with no animosity at all.

Another facet of their upbringing was a realization that whatever they gained as a result of their hard work would not come without toil, and their concern for finally becoming American citizens seemed to be tantamount to receiving a good education. Charles J. Cabibi remembered that "children of Italians made a life for themselves and they did it their way. Nobody lifted them up in any way. Italian families worked and worked." Donald Gennaro added, "They came over here and made a way for themselves."

The instances of Italians working hard to make their way in the New World seem to escape the younger generations of Italians, who do not seem to be proud of their Italian heritage or don't place much stock in the struggles of their ancestors. Additionally, the understanding on the younger Italians' part of the hard work needed to become Americans falls to the wayside due to daily concerns of family and job. This concerns the older Italians of the area because they feel their legacy of hard work and their efforts to become American citizens will be forgotten. "It is very difficult to get younger Italians interested in organizations that preserve the history," Ms. Regina Bertolino, president of the East Jefferson Italian American Association, claimed. "They just don't seem to care or don't have the time."

In any given year, thousands of visitors from all over the world journey to Louisiana to experience the rich culture, food, atmosphere and history only that state can claim as its own. In New Orleans today, a monument stands as a reminder to future generations of the contribution made by Italian Americans in Louisiana. The Piazza d'Italia, erected at the corner of South Peters Street and Poydras Avenue before the 1984 World Exposition, demonstrated to the world the cohesiveness of different cultures in Louisiana. Joe Maselli, founder of the American Italian Cultural Center; Joseph Cannizaro, a local businessman; and Dr. Nick Accardo, a respected orthopedic consultant, were instrumental in seeing the monument completed in time for tourists visiting the exposition to understand the importance of Italian culture in the area. After completion of the project, it stood as the "greatest edifice to Italians in America," according to Accardo. Indeed, it is a structure that embodies everything Italian, even some architectural reminders from the home country, commemorating the settlement in Louisiana of Italian forefathers who came to the United States.

At the turn of the millennium, Joe Maselli again became involved with a different project altogether—one that honored not just Italians but every immigrant who braved the journey to the New World. In Woldenberg Park, just off Conti Street near the Mississippi River in New Orleans, stands a statue entitled *Monument to the Immigrant*. Erected in 2002, this sculpture stands as a poignant reminder of the weary travelers who saw New Orleans as a gateway to the rest of the country. Some would move on, while others

Monument to the Immigrant, erected at the suggestion of Italian American community leader Joseph Maselli. *Courtesy of the author.*

stayed and populated the area with their distinctive cultures. The monument depicts a young father, his wife holding a baby and a young son at their side. This could portray most immigrant families who made their way to the United States in the nineteenth and early twentieth centuries. Their faces clearly depict the apprehension and fear they surely experienced as pilgrims in a strange land. New surroundings, an atmosphere indifferent to Italian customs and culture and an evolutionary prejudice made the Italian immigrants' transition to becoming American citizens especially difficult—more so than for most immigrants seeking the golden opportunity of freedom in America.

Bibliography

Primary Sources

Albano family member (anonymous). Author interview. July 6, 2011, Metairie, LA.

American Italian Cultural Center Oral History Collection. Sal Serio Sr., Curator. New Orleans.

Angola State Penitentiary Records. P 1980-353, 63761–64. Angola Book NS.11.

Autopsy Report of Anthony Sciambra, May 16, 1912, No. 609. Louisiana Collection/New Orleans City Archives, Irene Wainwright, Archivist.

Baron Fava to Secretary of State Olney, December 31, 1896, Washington, D.C. FRUS, 411–12

Baron Fava to Secretary Olney, December 31, 1896. Washington, D.C., FRUS, 412–417.

Bertolino, Regina. Author interview. February 19, 2013, St. Rose, LA.

Consul Corté to Baron Fava, March 15, 1891, New Orleans. In "Correspondence in Relation to the Killing of Prisoners in New Orleans, March 14, 1891." Historic New Orleans Collection, Williams Research Center, New Orleans.

Consul Corté to Baron Fava, New Orleans, No. 12. In "Correspondence in Relation to the Killing of Prisoners in New Orleans, March 14, 1891," 14. Historic New Orleans Collection, Williams Research Center, New Orleans.

Consul Corté to grand jury of New Orleans, November 13, 1890, New Orleans. In "Correspondence in Relation to the Killing of Prisoners in New Orleans, March 14, 1891." Historic New Orleans Collection, Williams Research Center, New Orleans.

Coroner's Inquest of Joseph and Catherine Maggio, Parish of Orleans, City of New Orleans, No. 295–96, May 23, 1918. Louisiana Collection/New Orleans City Archives, New Orleans Public Library, Loyola Branch. Irene Wainwright, Archivist.

Correspondence in Relation to the Killing of Prisoners in New Orleans on March 14, 1891. Washington, D.C.: Government Printing Office, 1891. Historic New Orleans Collection, Williams Research Center, New Orleans.

BIBLIOGRAPHY

Diary of T.C.W. Ellis. Ellis Family Papers, July 24, 1908. LSU Libraries, Hill Memorial Research Library, Louisiana State University. Manuscript Collection. Judy Bolton, Archivist.

Forty-eighth Congress, Session II, Chapter 164. Washington, D.C., February 26, 1885, 382.

Gennaro, Donald. Author interview. January 31, 2013, Metairie, LA.

Governor Francis T. Nicholls to Secretary of State James Blaine, December 2, 1890, Baton Rouge. In "Correspondence in Relation to the Killing of Prisoners in New Orleans, March 14, 1891," 9. Historic New Orleans Collection, Williams Research Center, New Orleans.

Governor Nicholls to Secretary Blaine, October 28, 1890, Baton Rouge, No. 2. In "Correspondence in Relation to the Killing of Prisoners in New Orleans, March 14, 1891." Historic New Orleans Collection, Williams Research Center, New Orleans.

Harris, William A. *Louisiana Products, Resources and Attractions: A Synopsis of Reliable Information Concerning the State.* New Orleans: E.A. Brandao & Co., Printers, 1885.

Hirsch, Dr. Arnold R., professor of history, University of New Orleans. Author interview. March 5, 2007.

Homicide Reports, Department of Police, New Orleans, 1911–19. New Orleans City Archives, New Orleans Public Library, Special Collections. Irene Wainwright, Archivist.

"Injustice to Italian Laborers." In *Messages and Papers of the Presidents, 1789–1897, Benjamin Harrison.* www.bklyn-geneology-info.com/Ethnic/Ital.Injustice.html.

Interview with Charles E. Cabbibi by Joseph Maselli. August 25, 1981, New Orleans. American Italian Cultural Center Oral History Collection, New Orleans.

Interview with Dr. Nick Accardo by Joseph Maselli, March 12, 1981, New Orleans. American Italian Cultural Center Oral History Collection, New Orleans.

James G. Blaine to Francis T. Nicholls, October 21, 1890, Washington D.C. No. 1. In "Correspondence in Relation to the Killing of Prisoners in New Orleans, March 14, 1891." Historic New Orleans Collection, Williams Research Center, New Orleans.

Jordano, Skip. Author interview. April 13, 2013, Folsom, LA.

Kemp, John R., ed. *Martin Behrman of New Orleans: Memoirs of a City Boss.* Baton Rouge: Louisiana State University Press, 1977.

Letter from J.H. Porterfield and A.C. Rulafson to Mayor Joseph A. Shakspeare, March 17, 1891, San Francisco, CA. Mayor Joseph A. Shakspeare Papers, Historic New Orleans Collection, Williams Research Center, New Orleans.

Letter from W.R. Coats to Mayor Joseph Shakspeare, May 19, 1891, Kalamazoo, MI. Mayor Joseph A. Shakspeare Papers, Historic New Orleans Collection, Williams Research Center, New Orleans.

Louisiana Constitution of 1898, Art. 197, Section 3. New Orleans: M.J. Hearsey Convention Printer, 1898.

Louisiana Sugar Planter's Association Minutes. New Orleans, January 3, 1878–June 9, 1881. Hill Memorial Library, Louisiana Collection, Louisiana State University Library.

Morrison, J. Chronegk. *Louisiana and Its Resources: The State of the Future.* Baton Rouge: Advocate, Official Journal of Louisiana, 1886.

Official Journal of the Louisiana Constitutional Convention. New Orleans: M.J. Hearsey, Convention Printer, 1898.

Postcard from T. Garland to Mayor Joseph Shakspeare, May 17, 1891, New York. Mayor Joseph A. Shakspeare Papers, Historic New Orleans Collection, Williams Research Center, New Orleans.

"Report of George W. Flynn, Supervisor of Registration for the Parish of Orleans." December 15, 1890, New Orleans, FRUS.

Report of Immigration to the General Assembly of Louisiana. New Orleans: A.L. Lee, State Printers, 1869.

"Report of the Committee of the Fifty" 49, May 15, 1891, in *Documents Relating to the Killing of the Prisoners on March 14, 1891.* Historic New Orleans Collection, New Orleans.

"Report of the Grand Jury as to the Killing in the New Orleans Parish Prison of Certain Persons Charged with the Murder of Chief of Police Hennessy." May 5, 1891, 48, 88. In "Correspondence in Relation to the Killing of Prisoners in New Orleans, March 14, 1891." Historic New Orleans Collection, Williams Research Center, New Orleans.

Secretary of State Olney to Baron Fava, November 27, 1896, Washington, D.C. FRUS, 407.

Spinato, Angelo J., Jr. Author interview. March 29, 2013, Metairie, LA.

State ex rel. v. The Judge of the Criminal District Court, Division A. 42 La. Ann 1089, 8 So. 277 (La. 1890), 1091.

State v. Rini, et al. 95 So. 400 (La. 1922).

Treaties and Conventions Concluded Between the United States and Other Powers. Washington, D.C.: Government Printing Office, 1871.

United States Immigration Commission (1907–1910): Part 24: Recent Immigrants in Agriculture, Vol. I. Washington, D.C.: Government Printing Office, 1911.

Warmoth, Henry Clay. *War, Politics, and Reconstruction: Stormy Days in Louisiana.* New York: Negro University Press, 1970.

William Grant to U.S. Attorney General W.H.H. Miller, April 27, 1891, New Orleans. In "Correspondence in Relation to the Killing of Prisoners in New Orleans, March 14, 1891." Historic New Orleans Collection, Williams Research Center, New Orleans.

NEWSPAPERS

Advocate Sunday Magazine, Baton Rouge, LA
Baton Rouge Weekly Advocate, Baton Rouge, LA
Daily Crescent, New Orleans
Daily Picayune, New Orleans
Inter Ocean, Chicago
Los Angeles Times
Louisiana Sugar Bowl
New Orleans Bee
New Orleans Bulletin
New Orleans Commercial Bulletin

New Orleans Item
New Orleans Mascot
New Orleans Times
New York Times
Salt Lake Tribune
San Francisco Bulletin
St. Bernard Voice, Chalmette, LA
Times Democrat, New Orleans
Times Picayune, New Orleans
Twin Falls News, Twin Falls, Iowa

U.S. CENSUS REPORTS

U.S. Census Office. *Eighth Census of the United States, 1860, Part I.* Washington, D.C.: Government Printing Office, 1864.

————. *Eleventh Census of the United States, 1890, Part I.* Washington, D.C.: Government Printing Office, 1895.

————. *Ninth Census of the United States, 1870, Part I.* Washington, D.C.: Government Printing Office, 1872.

————. *Tenth Census of the United States, 1880, Part I.* Washington, D.C.: Government Printing Office, 1882.

————. *Thirteenth Census of the United States, 1910, Part I.* Washington, D.C.: Government Printing Office, 1911.

SECONDARY SOURCES

Books

Allen, Frederick. *A Decent, Orderly Lynching: The Montana Vigilantes.* Norman: Oklahoma University Press, 2004.

Allen, James, Hilton Als, Congressman John Lewis and Leon F. Zitwack, eds. *Without Sanctuary: Lynch Photography in America.* Santa Fe, NM: Twin Palms Publishers, 2002.

Arnesen, Eric. *Waterfront Workers of New Orleans: Race, Class, and Politics.* Oxford, UK: University of Oxford Press, 1991.

Asbury, Herbert. *The French Quarter: An Informal History of the New Orleans Underworld.* New York: Garden City Publishing, 1938.

Ayers, Edward. *The Promise of the New South: Life After Reconstruction.* Oxford, UK: Oxford University Press, 1992.

Baiamonte, John V. *Spirit of Vengeance: Nativism and Louisiana Justice, 1921–1924.* Baton Rouge: Louisiana State University Press, 1986.

Bartlett, Napier. *Military Record of Louisiana.* Baton Rouge: Louisiana State University Press, 1964.

Beals, Carleton. *Brass Knuckle Crusade: The Great Know-Nothing Conspiracy, 1820–1860.* New York: Hastings House Publishers, 1960.

Black, Henry Campbell. *Black's Law Dictionary.* St. Paul, MN: West Publishing Company, 1990.

Borsella, Cristogianni. *On Persecution, Identity, and Activism: Aspects of the Italian-American Experience from Late 19ᵗʰ Century to Today.* Boston: Dante Press, 2005.

Boulard, Garry. *Huey Long Invades New Orleans: The Siege of a City, 1934–1936.* New Orleans: Pelican Publishing Company, 1998.

————. *Louis Prima: Music in American Life, Just a Gigolo.* Urbana, IL: University of Chicago Press, 2002.

Bourg, David F., and L. Edward Purcell. *The Almanac of World War I.* Lexington: University of Kentucky Press, 1998.

Brands, H.W. *TR: The Last Romantic.* New York: Basic Books, 1997.

Brundage, W. Fitzhugh, ed. *Under Sentence of Death: Lynching in the South*. Chapel Hill: University of North Carolina Press, 1997.

Campbell, Anne. *Louisiana: The History of an American State*. Atlanta: Clairmont Press, 2007.

Chandler, David L. *Brothers in Blood: The Rise of the Criminal Brotherhoods*. New York: E.P. Dutton & Co. Inc., 1975.

Davis, John. *Mafia Kingfish: Carlos Marcello and the Assassination of John F. Kennedy*. New York: McGraw-Hill Publishers, 1989.

Di Donato, Pietro. *Immigrant Saint: The Life of Mother Cabrini*. New York: McGraw Hill, 1960.

Douglas, John E., and Mark Olshaker. *Obsessions: The F.B.I.'s Legendary Profiler Probes the Psyches of Killers, Rapists, and Stalkers and Their Victims and Tells How to Fight Back*. New York: Scribner Books, 1998.

Dray, Philip. *At the Hands of Persons Unknown: The Lynching of Black America*. Montclair, NJ: Random House, 2002.

DuBois, W.E.B. *The Souls of Black Folk*. Edited by Henry Louis Gates Jr. and Teri Hume Olivier. New York: W.W. Norton & Company, 1999.

Federal Writers' Project, Works Progress Administration in the City of New York. *The Italians of New York: A Survey*. New York: Random House, 1969.

Gambino, Richard. *Blood of My Blood: The Dilemma of the Italian-Americans*. Garden City, NY: Anchor Press/Doubleday, 1974.

————. *Vendetta: The True Story of the Worst Lynching in America*. Garden City, NY: Doubleday & Company, 1977.

Garvey, Joan B., and Mary Lou Widner. *A Beautiful Crescent: A History of New Orleans*. New Orleans: Garmer Press, 1984.

Gill, James. *Lords of Misrule: Mardi Gras and the Politics of Race in New Orleans*. Jackson: University Press of Mississippi, 1997.

Guglielmo, Thomas A. *White on Arrival: Italians, Race, Color, and Power in Chicago, 1890–1945*. New York: Oxford University Press, 2003.

Haas, Edward F. *Political Leadership in a Southern City: New Orleans in the Progressive Era, 1896–1902*. Ruston, LA: McGinty Publications, 1988.

Hair, William Ivy. *Bourbonism and the Agrarian Protest: Louisiana Politics, 1877–1900*. Baton Rouge: Louisiana State University Press, 1969.

Hersch, Charles. *Subversive Sounds: Race and the Birth of Jazz in New Orleans, 1885–1963*. Chicago: University of Chicago Press, 2009.

Hicks, John D. *The Populist Revolt: A History of the Farmers' Alliance and the People's Party*. Minneapolis: University of Minnesota Press, 1931.

Hyde, Samuel C., Jr. *Pistols and Politics: The Dilemma of Democracy in Louisiana's Florida Parishes, 1810–1899*. Baton Rouge: Louisiana State University Press, 1996.

Jacobsen, Matthew Frye. *Whiteness of a Different Color: European Immigrants and the Alchemy of Race*. Cambridge, MA: Harvard University Press, 1988.

Kane, Harnett T. *Huey Long's Louisiana Hayride: The American Rehearsal for Dictatorship, 1928–1940*. Gretna, LA: Pelican Publishing Company, 1970.

LaFore, Laurence. *The Long Fuse: An Interpretation of the Origins of World War I*. New York: J.B. Lippincott and Company Publishers, 1965.

Leeds, Christopher. *The Unification of Italy*. London: Wayland Publishers, 1974.

Lonn, Ella. *Reconstruction in Louisiana after 1868*. New York: Russell & Russell, 1918.

Lord, Eliot. *The Italian in America*. New York: B.F. Buck & Company, 1905.

Jakubowsky, Maxim, and Nathan Braund, eds. *The Mammoth Book of Jack the Ripper*. New York: Carroll & Graff Publishers, 1999.

Magnaghi, Russell. "Louisiana's Italian Immigrants Before 1870." In *A Refuge for All Ages: Immigration in Louisiana History*. Vol. 10. Edited by Carl A. Brasseaux. Lafayette: Center for Louisiana Studies, University of Southwestern Louisiana, 1996.

Margavio, A.V., and Jerome J. Salamone. *Bread and Respect: The Italians of Louisiana*. New Orleans: Pelican Publishing, 2002.

Maselli, Joseph, and Dominic Candeloro. *Italians in New Orleans*. Charleston, SC: Arcadia Publishing, 2004.

McCrary, Gregory O., and Katherine Ramsland. *The Unknown Darkness: Profiling the Predators Among Us*. New York: Harper Torch Publishing, 2004.

Morgan, Thomas. *Historic Photos of New Orleans Jazz*. Nashville, TN: Turner Publishing, 2009.

Nelli, Humbert S. *The Business of Crime: Italians and Syndicate Crime in the United States*. Chicago: University of Chicago Press, 1976.

———. *From Immigrants to Ethnics: The Italian Americans*. Oxford, UK: Oxford University Press, 1983.

Overdyke, W. Darrell. *The Know-Nothing Party of the South*. Baton Rouge: Louisiana State University Press, 1950.

Palmer, R.R., and Joel Colton. *A History of the Modern World*. New York: McGraw-Hill, 1995.

Paret, Peter. "Alfred Thayer Mahan: The Naval Historian." In *Makers in Modern Strategy: From Machiavelli to the Nuclear Age*. Princeton, NJ: Princeton University Press, 1986.

Perry, Howard. *Political Tendencies in Louisiana*. Baton Rouge: Louisiana State University Press, 1957.

Pfeifer, Michael. *Rough Justice: Lynching and American Society, 1814–1974*. Urbana: University of Illinois Press, 2004.

Rable, George C. *But There Was No Peace: The Role of Violence in the Politics of Reconstruction*. Athens: University of Georgia, 1984.

Raper, Arthur F. *The Tragedy of Lynching*. Montclair, NJ: Patterson Smith, 1969.

Riall, Lucy. "Garibaldi and the South." In *Italy and the Nineteenth Century*. Edited by John A. Davis. Oxford, UK: Oxford University Press, 2000.

Roediger, David. *Working Toward Whiteness: How America's Immigrants Became White*. New York: Basic Books, 2005.

Rolle, Andrew. *The Italian Americans: Troubled Roots*. New York: MacMillan Publishing Company, 1980.

Sacher, John M. *A Perfect War of Politics: Parties, Politicians, and Democracy in Louisiana, 1824–1861*. Baton Rouge: Louisiana State University Press, 2003.

Saxon, Lyle, Edward Dreyer and Robert Tallant. *Gumbo Ya-Ya: A Collection of Louisiana Folktales*. Gretna, LA: Pelican Publishing Company, 1991.

Scarpaci, Jean Ann. *Italian Immigrants in Louisiana's Sugar Parishes: Recruitment, Labor Conditions, and Community Relations 1880–1910*. New York: Arno Press, 1980.

Schindler, Allen P. "The Setting for Recent Politics." In *The Louisiana Purchase Bicentennial Series in Louisiana History*. Vol. VII: *Louisiana Politics and Paradoxes of*

Reaction and Reform, 1877–1928. Edited by Matthew Schott. Lafayette: Center for Louisiana Studies, University of Louisiana, 2000.

Sergi, Guiseppi. *The Mediterranean Race.* N.p., 1895, 1901.

Shugg, Roger. *Origins of Class Struggle in the South.* Baton Rouge: Louisiana State University Press, 1939.

Smith, Denis Mack. *A History of Sicily: Modern Sicily Since 1813.* New York: Viking Press, 1968.

———. *Victor Emanuel, Cavour, and the Risorgimento.* London: Oxford University Press, 1971.

Smith, Tom. *The Crescent City Lynchings: The Murder of Chief Hennessy, the New Orleans "Mafia" Trials, and the Parish Prison Mob.* Guilford, CT: Lyons Press, 2007.

Somers, Robert. *The Southern States Since the War, 1870–1871.* Introduction by Malcolm C. McMillan. Tuscaloosa: University of Alabama Press, 1965.

Sondern, Frederic, Jr. *Brotherhood of Evil: The Mafia.* New York: Farrar, Strauss, & Cudahy, 1983.

Soulé, Leon Cyprian. *The Know-Nothing Party of New Orleans: A Reappraisal.* Baton Rouge: Louisiana Historical Association, 1962.

Southern Horrors and Other Writings: The Anti-Lynching Campaign of Ida B. Wells, 1891–1900. Edited by Jacqueline Jones Royster. The Bedford Series in History and Culture. New York: Bedford/St. Martin's Press, 1997.

Sullivan, Brian R. "The Strategy of the Decisive Weight, 1882–1922." In *The Making of Strategy: Rulers, States, and War.* Edited by Williamson Murray, Macgregor Knox and Alvin Bernstein. Cambridge, UK: Cambridge University Press, 1994.

Tallant, Robert. *Ready to Hang: Seven Famous New Orleans Murders.* New York: Harper & Brothers Publishers, 1952.

Thomas, Evan. *The War Lovers: Roosevelt, Lodge, Hearst, and the Rush to Empire, 1898.* New York: Little, Brown, and Company, 2010.

Wall, Bennett, et al. *Louisiana: A History.* Arlington Heights, IL, 1984.

Wells, Ida B. *Southern Horrors: Lynch Law and All Its Phases.* New York: New York Age Print, 1892.

White, Richard D. *Kingfish: The Reign of Huey P. Long.* New York: Random House, 2006.

Williamson, Samuel R., Jr. *Austria-Hungary and the Origins of the First World War.* New York: St. Martin's Press, 1991.

Williams, T. Harry. *Huey Long.* New York: Alfred A. Knopf, Publishers, 1969.

Journal Articles

Abramowitz, Jack. "The Negro in the Populist Movement." *Journal of Negro History* 38, no. 3 (July 1953).

Botein, Barbara. "The Hennessy Case: An Episode in Anti-Italian Nativism." *Louisiana Historical Journal* 20, no. 3 (Summer 1979).

Brandfon, Robert L. "The End of Immigration to the Cotton Fields." *Mississippi Valley Historical Review* 50, no. 4 (March 1964): 591–611.

Brundage, W. Fitzhugh. "Conclusion: Reflections on Lynching Scholarship." *American Nineteenth Century History* 6, no. 3 (September 2005).

Cometti, Elizabeth. "Trends in Italian Immigration." *Western Political Quarterly* 11, no. 4 (December 1958): 820–34.

Coxe, John E. "The New Orleans Mafia Incident." *Louisiana Historical Journal* 20, no. 4 (October 1937).

———. "The New Orleans Mafia Incident." Unpublished master's thesis, Louisiana State University, 1928.

Cunningham, George. "The Italian as a Hindrance to White Solidarity in Louisiana, 1890–1898." *Journal of Negro History* 50, no. 1 (January 1965).

D'Agostino, Peter. "Craniums, Criminals, and the 'Cursed Race': Italian Anthropology in U.S. Racial Thought." *Comparative Studies of Society and History* 44, no. 2 (April 2002): 319–43.

Dethloff, Henry Clay. "Populism and Reform in Louisiana." Unpublished dissertation, University of Missouri, PhD, 1964.

Fleming, Walter L. "Immigration to the Southern States." *Political Science Quarterly* (June 1905).

Haas, Edward F. "New Orleans on the Half-Shell: The Maestri Era, 1936–1946." *Louisiana History: The Journal of the Louisiana Historical Association* 13, no. 3 (Summer 1972): 283–310.

Inverarity, James M. "Populism and Lynching in Louisiana, 1889–1896: A Test of Erickson's Theory of Relationship Between the Boundary Crisis and Repressive Justice." *American Sociological Review* 41, no. 2 (April 1976): 355–58.

Jaeger, Daniela. "The Worst 'White Lynching': Elites v. Italians in New Orleans, 1891." Unpublished master's thesis, University of New Orleans, 2001.

Johnson, David A. "Vigilance and the Law: The Moral Authority of Popular Justice in the Far West." *American Quarterly* 33, no. 5 (August 1995): 558–86.

Kendall, John. "Who Killa Da Chief?" *Louisiana Historical Quarterly* 22, no. 2 (April 1939).

Margavio, A.V., and J. Lambert Molyneaux. "Residential Segregation of Italians in New Orleans and Selected American Cities." *Journal of Louisiana Studies* 12, no. 4 (Winter 1973).

Simms-Brown, R. Jean. "Populism and Black Americans: Constructive or Destructive?" *Journal of Negro History* 65, no. 4 (Autumn 1980).

Sullivan, Mary Louise. "Mother Cabrini: Missionary to Italian Immigrants." *U.S. Catholic Historian* 6, no. 4 (Fall 1987).

"United States and Italy." *American Advocate of Peace and Arbitration* 53, no. 3 (April 1880).

White, Melvin Johnson. "Populism in Louisiana in the Nineties." *Mississippi Valley Historical Review* 5, no. 1 (June 1918).

Magazine Articles

"The Mafia in Sicily." *Littell's Living Age* 74, no. 2449 (June 6, 1891): 632–34.

Morgan, Appleton. "What Shall We Do with the Dago?" *Popular Science Monthly* 38, no. 2 (December 1890): 172–79.

Ross, Edward Allworth. "Italians in America." *Century Magazine* 66 (May–October 1914): 440–42.

Shields, Alan. "The Axeman of New Orleans." *Detective Cases Magazine* (April 1991): 19, 37–40.

Wolfson, L. "Italian Secret Societies." *Littell's Living Age* 74, no. 2449 (June 6, 1891): 621–24.

Index

About the Author

Alan G. Gauthreaux was born and raised in the New Orleans area. Mr. Gauthreaux holds bachelor's and master's degrees in history from the University of New Orleans and has been researching, writing and lecturing about a variety of topics in local and national history for over twenty years. His previous works may be found in *Civil War Times Magazine*, the *Louisiana Historical Journal* and *History Magazine*.

Courtesy of Lisa L. Gauthreaux.